Short & Sweet

Desserts and Beverages In Less Than Thirty Minutes!

Favorite Recipes® Press

Printed on Recycled Paper

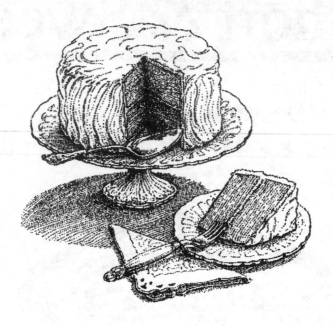

Great American Opportunities, Inc./Favorite Recipes® Press

Essayist: Yvonne Martin Kidd
Cover Photograph: Hershey Foods Corporation

This cookbook is a collection of our favorite recipes,
which are not necessarily original recipes.

Library of Congress Number: 92-7465
ISBN: 0-87197-330-8

Printed in the United States of America
First Printing: 1992

CONTENTS

See pages 155–161 for nutritional information of individual recipes.

THE THREE R'S OF ECOLOGY

Introducing the Three R's

REDUCE REUSE RECYCLE

Things sure have changed since I was a kid.

Back in the sixties when I grew up, the three R's referred to reading, 'riting, and 'rithmetic. Classrooms did not have calculators or computers. Kids still walked home for a hot lunch, or else carried one with them in a thermos and metal lunchbox.

In those days, a mere thirty years ago, *convenience* was not yet part of the everyday vocabulary. Mothers had time to prepare meals and tackle household chores, since raising the kids was usually the only job they held. The frozen food section of the supermarket was small, limited mostly to ice cream and vegetables. A trip to McDonald's (if you were lucky enough to have one in your town) was a special occasion rather than a regular habit.

We've come a long way since then, and I, for one, am glad that we have. Technology has brought us thousands of products which make our lives easier. How did we ever live without the microwave oven? What did we do before neatly packaged convenience foods? How did we manage household chores before the advent of squeeze and spray bottles? For making our lives easier and for giving us more free time, I say "Hooray!" for technology.

On the other hand, every silver lining has a cloud.

Technology has given us so much, and yet the sad truth is that it hasn't given us a way to deal with all the garbage created by these products. Very simply put, there's too much trash.

For every microwave meal that moves from the supermarket freezer to the table, a carton or tray will find its way to the trash can. For every fast-food hamburger ordered, a container must be disposed of. For every bottle of window cleaner or furniture polish used, a plastic or glass container will be thrown away.

Technology's trash is piling up on us. Landfill space—places to put all the garbage we produce—is running out. Unfortunately, the garbage has to go somewhere. And so it is starting to flow over into our neighborhoods, scenic highways, and the oceans.

What's the answer? We need to adopt a new set of three R's, designed to decrease the amount of garbage we produce. The three R's of ecology are *REDUCE*, *REUSE*, and *RECYCLE*.

REDUCE. We must reduce the amount of garbage we produce by making better choices up front. Whenever possible, we need to choose less instead of more, durable instead of trendy, permanent rather than disposable. When given a choice, we should select environmentally friendly items over nonbiodegradable plastics that will clutter the landscape long after we're gone.

REUSE. Sometimes we throw things out that still have a useful life. We should be creative and ask ourselves: "Can this item be repaired? Can it be used for something else?" If the answer is yes, we've just saved valuable space in the trash can.

RECYCLE. We should get into the habit of recycling items we can no longer use. Whether it's clothes or shoes, small appliances or other household objects, there may be another family or charity that would consider our "trash" to be their "treasure." In the case of newspapers, cans, glass bottles, and plastic containers, most of us have easy access to a recycling center where such items can be reprocessed and used once again. Once you get into the habit, the three R's of ecology are easy to follow. If each of us started practicing them, even just a bit, we could put a big dent in the problem of too much trash.

Putting the Three R's to Work

Think back to how your grandmother ran her household. Chances are, she used washcloths and sponges and dishtowels instead of paper towels. There were probably no disposable razors, diapers, pens, or cigarette lighters around her house. She would leave empty glass milk bottles outside her door to be collected by the milkman and reused. Maybe she even had kitchen drawers filled with used wrapping paper, aluminum foil, and string to be used on future projects.

Your grandmother didn't know it, but she was putting the three R's of ecology into practice. The only difference was that she would have called it good old-fashioned common sense.

Here are some common-sense suggestions for putting the three R's to work around your house.

EDUCE

*Don't buy things you really don't need. Before you shop—for groceries or toiletries or clothes or shoes—take stock of what you already have and make a shopping list.

*Reduce the amount of packaging you purchase. When possible, buy products such as rice, grains, pasta, and vegetables *in bulk*, to eliminate excess packaging.

*Reduce your reliance on store-bought foods. Start a small vegetable garden to grow tomatoes, herbs, and squash. Make your own microwave meals by doubling your favorite dinner recipes and freezing portions for later.

*Avoid the impulse to buy packaged "junk foods." Keep snacks readily available in the refrigerator—vegetable sticks, cheese cubes, yogurt, good bread. Grill hamburger patties and freeze them to have food ready for quick heating in the microwave.

*Avoid Styrofoam packaging and products. Select fast-food restaurants that use paper and cardboard containers. Purchase eggs in paper cartons. Choose disposable paper plates instead of plastic.

*Buy things that are durable and will last. Avoid products (clothing, small kitchen appliances, toiletries) that may be "in" today and "out" tomorrow.

REUSE

*When possible, avoid reliance on plastic wraps and aluminum foil. Buy a good set of storage containers for leftovers. Stock up on containers that can go from the freezer directly into the microwave.

*Help prevent products from wearing out. Resole and polish shoes to keep them fresh. Buy replacement parts for appliances. Use products according to the directions.

*Purchase items that are reusable rather than disposable. Pack lunch in a lunchbox rather than a paper bag. When possible, use real razors, refillable pens, rechargeable batteries, and cloth diapers, dishtowels, and washcloths.

*Carry a canvas or string bag to the store rather than using new bags each time, or reuse the grocery and department store bags which you received with your last purchase.

*Use ceramic mugs and reusable cups for work or school.

*Reuse plastic and glass containers, squeeze and spray bottles that originally came with food and nonhazardous household cleaning products.

RECYCLE

*Recycle glass, aluminum, metal cans, newspapers, and certain types of plastic. (Check your local recycling center to find out exactly what they'll take and hours of collection.) Set up a location in your home or garage to store items for recycling, taking care to avoid potential heat sources such as the furnace, water heater, and dryer.

*Create a space in the garage or a spare closet to collect unneeded items such as clothing, toys, appliances, and shelf-stable foodstuffs, for charity or a garage sale.

*When purchasing stationery, greeting cards, photocopy paper, and other packaged goods, buy products made of recycled materials.

*Start a compost pile in which to recycle kitchen scraps, lawn and garden waste, and other organic garbage.

Family Projects for Fun and Profit

Practicing the three R's doesn't have to be a chore. Here are some ideas to make it fun and easy for the whole family.

Operation Cleanup

Take a trip to a local park or beach. Pack a picnic lunch and plan some games for the whole family. In addition to Frisbee or croquet, play a game called Operation Cleanup. Break up into teams, then give each team an area to explore and a set amount of time in which to do it. The "exploration" should include picking up all trash, including paper, unbroken glass, and aluminum cans. At the end of the time period, the team with the most trash wins! (Make sure to recycle all the trash you can.)

Spring-Cleaning Garage Sale

Clear a large space in the garage or playroom in which to pile items for a garage sale. Ask each family member to go through closets for clothing, shoes, toys, games, household appliances, toiletries, and other assorted knickknacks that are no longer in use. Select a sunny spring weekend for the garage sale and place an inexpensive ad in the local newspaper.

Use the money collected from the garage sale to buy something the whole family can enjoy, such as an evening at the movies, a special dinner, or a new game.

Dinner for the Homeless

With the family, take an hour on a Saturday afternoon to clean out the kitchen cupboards of canned goods or unopened staples that have not been used in the past twelve months or will not be used in the near future. Pack these items into paper bags and, as a group, deliver them to a local homeless shelter. You may even want to ask if you can stay and help prepare or serve dinner. Your efforts will be well rewarded.

Handmade Christmas

This Christmas, in addition to store-bought gifts, ask each family member to hand-make at least one gift for another member of the family. Consider things that can be baked, such as cookies and brownies; presents that can be sewn, such as pillows or pin cushions; or things that can be made in the garage workshop, such as a "recycled playhouse" using leftover materials—scrap wood, carpeting, and wallpaper.

Learning from Experience

In ecology, as in most things, experience is often the best teacher. If you think about it, you've probably had an experience or two that help you better understand the three R's and how they can be incorporated into your life. For example:

Maybe you reviewed your grocery bill and concluded you were spending far too much money on prepared foods, and the answer was to prepare more meals from scratch. (*Reduce*)

Maybe you had decided to buy a new vacuum cleaner (or bicycle, or blender), but your next-door neighbor was able to fix your old one. (*Reuse*)

Maybe you visited a homeless shelter and realized there are many people who need items you've been throwing away. (*Recycle*)

My valuable experience happened when I was fourteen years old. I call it *The Lesson of the Sturdy Shoes*.

THE LESSON OF THE STURDY SHOES

I always thought my mother was eccentric. You see, she had this thing for sturdy shoes.

Each year, she would take me to the local department store to buy my single annual pair of sturdy shoes. Although my mouth would water over the brightly colored pumps and the patent-leather high heels that were in fashion, my mother barely even noticed them. Instead, she directed the salesman to bring out whatever he had in a well-made shoe, size 5½ B, in brown leather, with a low heel.

She might just as well have asked for the dullest, drabbest, most dreary-looking pair of shoes in the whole store, because those were always the ones we went home with.

"Sturdy" might have been just fine when I was in grade school, but it certainly would not do for a budding teenager. The year I turned fourteen, I realized that all my friends had me beat in the fashion department—especially Laurie, with her perky brown hair, UltraBrite smile, and extensive wardrobe. I knew I could never completely catch up to Laurie, but I was determined to try. And I would start at the bottom, by getting rid of the sturdy shoes.

Surprisingly, it didn't take long to convince my mother. That year, she agreed to let me buy as many pairs of shoes as I wanted, so long as they didn't cost more than the single pair she would have chosen. In addition, I needed to understand that no matter which shoes I selected, they would have to last the entire school year.

I had a wonderful time at the discount shoe store. There were so many styles and colors to choose from! I emerged two hours later with three pairs of fashionable, contemporary, relatively inexpensive shoes, all of them made of patent leather. The first pair were brown-and-white sling-back shoes that tied in the front with a ribbon. The second and third pairs, simulating the look of saddle shoes, were navy blue and bright red.

For a few short weeks I was in shoe heaven. Then disillusionment set in.

11

The brown-and-white sling-backs were the first to go. It seemed that dainty slings, inch-and-a-half heels, and ribbons couldn't stand up to the tough pounding given them by an active teenager. Maybe it was the four-mile bike ride to and from school. Maybe it was the lunch-time basketball games. Whatever the cause, those shoes soon disintegrated.

I had two pairs of shoes left: bright red and navy blue. Unfortunately, neither of them matched the clothes I had in my wardrobe. The situation worsened, however, when the navy blue pair, the least objectionable match of the two, fell apart. I attributed this to faulty glue.

Mercifully, the red pair went quickly after that. I honestly can't remember if they wore out by themselves or if I helped them along. They met their demise in a dumpster behind the high school gym.

The school year wasn't even half over, and already I was back to wearing last year's scuffed but sturdy shoes. After a few weeks of this, my mother took pity on me. Eagerly I joined her on the trip to our local department store, where in unison we asked the salesman to bring us whatever he had in a well-made shoe, size 5½ B, in brown leather with a low heel.

My mother never said "I told you so." She let me learn the lesson of the sturdy shoes for myself.

The lesson is this: Durability is a virtue. It may not always be exciting, but it pays off in the selection of any item that you have to live with, day in and day out. Whether you're purchasing shoes or clothing, furniture or carpeting, automobiles or gardening tools, toiletries or small kitchen appliances, buy things that will last.

Today, as I reflect on our need to reduce that amount of garbage we produce by making better choices and eliminating extra purchases, I think of the sturdy shoes and chuckle. What I thought of as eccentric when I was fourteen years old has turned out to be smart, practical, even fashionable.

My mother knew it all along!

AWESOME ICE CREAM

Nutritional information for Awesome Ice Cream is on page 155.

BROWNIE BAKED ALASKA

1   9x13-inch pan uncut baked brownie
½ gallon vanilla ice cream, softened
6 egg whites
½ teaspoon cream of tartar
1 cup sugar

Spread brownie layer with ice cream to within ½ inch of edges. Freeze. Beat egg whites with cream of tartar in mixer bowl until foamy. Add sugar 1 tablespoon at a time, beating well after each addition until stiff and glossy. Spread over ice cream, sealing to edges. Bake at 500 degrees for 3 minutes or until browned. Serve immediately.

Yield: 12 servings.   **Prep Time:** 10 minutes plus freezing.

FROZEN BANANA SPLIT

1 cup graham cracker crumbs
4 bananas, sliced
½ gallon strawberry ice cream
1 cup chocolate chips
½ cup margarine
1⅓ cups evaporated milk
2 cups confectioners' sugar
8 ounces whipped topping
1 cup chopped walnuts

Sprinkle cracker crumbs into 9x13-inch dish. Top with banana slices. Spread ice cream over bananas. Freeze. Combine chocolate chips, margarine, evaporated milk and confectioners' sugar in saucepan. Bring to a boil, stirring constantly. Cool. Pour over ice cream. Spread with whipped topping. Sprinkle with walnuts.

Yield: 15 servings.   **Prep Time:** 15 minutes plus freezing.

BANANA-ICE CREAM PIE

2 bananas
1 baked 8-inch pie shell
2 cups vanilla ice cream, softened
½ cup milk
1   4-ounce package vanilla instant pudding mix

Slice bananas into pie shell. Combine ice cream, milk and pudding mix in bowl; mix well. Spoon over bananas. Chill for 2 hours. May omit bananas and substitute chocolate pudding mix for vanilla.

Yield: 6 servings.   **Prep Time:** 5 minutes plus chilling.

BUBBLE CROWN

1 cup water
½ cup butter
1 cup sifted flour
4 eggs
1 quart pistachio ice cream, softened
1 quart cherry ice cream, softened

Bring water and butter to a rolling boil in saucepan. Add flour all at once, stirring for 1 minute or until mixture leaves side of pan; remove from heat. Beat in eggs 1 at a time, beating until smooth after each addition. Drop by scant teaspoonfuls onto ungreased baking sheet. Bake at 425 degrees for 15 minutes or until golden brown; cool. Arrange ⅓ of the puffs in large tube pan. Layer pistachio ice cream over puffs. Top with half the remaining puffs, cherry ice cream and remaining puffs. Freeze until firm. Unmold onto serving plate. May use favorite flavors of ice cream.

Yield: 16 servings.   **Prep Time:** 20 minutes plus freezing.

BUTTER BRICKLE DESSERT

2 cups all-purpose flour
1/2 cup oats
1 cup chopped pecans
1/2 cup packed brown sugar
1/2 cup melted margarine
1 cup caramel sauce
1 pint vanilla ice cream

Combine flour, oats, pecans, brown sugar and margarine in bowl; mix well. Pat into thin layer on baking sheet. Bake at 400 degrees for 15 minutes. Crumble while hot. Sprinkle half the crumbs in 9x13-inch dish. Drizzle with half the caramel sauce. Spread ice cream over sauce. Sprinkle with remaining crumbs. Drizzle with remaining sauce. Freeze until firm.

Yield: 12 servings.   **Prep Time:** 25 minutes plus freezing.

CHERRY DELIGHT

36 Oreo cookies, crushed
1/2 cup margarine, softened
1/2 gallon vanilla ice cream
1 21-ounce can cherry pie filling
4 cups whipped topping
1/4 cup chocolate syrup
1/2 cup chopped pecans

Combine cookie crumbs and margarine in bowl; mix well. Press into 9x13-inch glass dish. Slice ice cream; arrange over crust. Layer pie filling and whipped topping over ice cream. Drizzle with chocolate syrup; sprinkle with pecans. Freeze, covered, until firm. Remove from freezer several minutes before serving.

Yield: 15 servings.   **Prep Time:** 10 minutes plus freezing.

CHOCOLATE ICE CRISPY PIE

½ cup HERSHEY'S syrup
⅓ cup HERSHEY'S Semi-sweet Chocolate Chips
2 cups crisp rice cereal   ¼ cup dairy sour cream
1 quart strawberry ice cream

Microwave syrup with chocolate chips in glass bowl on High for 45 seconds; mix well. Remove ¼ cup; set aside. Add cereal to remaining chocolate mixture; mix well. Press into buttered 8-inch pie plate. Freeze until firm. Fold sour cream into reserved chocolate mixture. Scoop ice cream into pie shell. Spoon chocolate sour cream over top. May substitute ½ cup coconut for ¼ cup cereal.

Yield: 6 servings.   **Prep Time:** 10 minutes plus freezing.

Photograph for this recipe is on the cover.

CHOCOLATE MALT ICE CREAM TORTE

1 cup finely crushed graham cracker crumbs
3 tablespoons sugar   1 teaspoon cinnamon
3 tablespoons melted margarine, cooled
2 tablespoons finely grated semisweet chocolate
½ gallon fudge ripple ice cream, softened
½ cup malted milk powder
4 ounces chocolate-covered malted
milk balls, coarsely chopped

Combine crumbs, sugar and cinnamon in bowl; mix well. Stir in margarine and chocolate until well mixed. Press onto bottom and halfway up side of greased springform pan. Combine ice cream and malted milk powder in bowl; beat until well blended. Spread over crumb mixture. Sprinkle with chopped malted milk balls, patting lightly into ice cream. Freeze, covered, until firm. Loosen from side of pan with knife dipped in hot water. Remove side of pan. Cut into wedges.

Yield: 12 servings.   **Prep Time:** 15 minutes plus freezing.

CRANBERRY ICE CREAM PIE

1 cup quick-cooking oats, toasted
1/2 cup packed brown sugar
1/2 cup coconut
1/3 cup melted margarine
1 quart vanilla ice cream, slightly softened
1   16-ounce can whole cranberry sauce
1 teaspoon grated lemon rind

Combine oats, brown sugar, coconut and margarine in bowl; mix well. Press over bottom and side of 9-inch pie plate. Chill for several minutes. Spoon ice cream into prepared pie shell. Combine cranberry sauce and lemon rind in bowl; mix well. Spread over pie. Serve immediately or freeze until firm.

Yield: 8 servings.   **Prep Time:** 10 minutes.

EASY ICE CREAM DESSERT

1 cup melted margarine
1/2 cup packed brown sugar
1/2 cup quick-cooking oats
2 cups flour
1 cup chopped pecans
1 1/2   8-ounce jars fudge sauce
1/2 gallon fudge ripple ice cream, softened

Mix margarine, brown sugar, oats, flour and pecans in bowl. Spread in 9x13-inch baking pan. Bake at 375 degrees for 10 minutes or until golden brown; cool. Crumble mixture. Sprinkle half the mixture into 9x13-inch dish. Spread with half the fudge sauce. Spread ice cream over fudge sauce. Top with remaining crumbs and fudge sauce. Freeze until firm.

Yield: 15 servings.   **Prep Time:** 20 minutes plus freezing.

CRISPY ICE CREAM ROLL

¼ cup melted margarine
1 16-ounce can vanilla frosting
¼ cup light corn syrup
5 cups crisp rice cereal
1 quart caramel pecan ice cream

Combine margarine, frosting and corn syrup in bowl; mix well. Stir in cereal; coat well. Press into waxed paper-lined 10x13-inch pan. Chill in freezer for 30 minutes. Spread ice cream over rice cereal mixture. Roll as for jelly roll. Freeze until firm. Cut into slices.

Yield: 10 servings.   **Prep Time:** 15 minutes plus freezing.

MINCEMEAT AND VANILLA ICE CREAM TORTE

3 tablespoons melted margarine
1¼ cups vanilla wafer crumbs
5 pints vanilla ice cream, softened
1 28-ounce jar mincemeat
1 cup sliced almonds, toasted

Mix margarine and vanilla wafer crumbs in bowl. Press onto bottom and side of greased 9-inch springform pan. Chill until firm. Combine ice cream and mincemeat in bowl; mix well. Spoon over prepared crust. Sprinkle with toasted almonds. Freeze, covered, until firm. Remove side of pan. Let stand at room temperature for 10 minutes.

Yield: 16 servings.   **Prep Time:** 15 minutes plus freezing.

*Substitute ice milk or frozen yogurt for ice cream
to reduce calories and fat.*

MOCHA PARFAIT PIE

1 7-ounce can sweetened coconut
1 cup finely chopped pecans
2 tablespoons all-purpose flour
1/2 cup melted margarine
1/2 gallon mocha coffee ice cream, softened
1/2 cup whipping cream, whipped
2 tablespoons grated chocolate

Combine coconut, pecans and flour in bowl; mix well. Stir in margarine. Press into pie plate. Bake at 375 degrees for 10 minutes or until golden brown; cool. Pack ice cream into crust. Top with whipped cream and grated chocolate.

Yield: 10 servings.   **Prep Time:** 20 minutes.

ORANGE TORTE

1/2 cup vanilla wafer crumbs
1 quart vanilla ice cream, softened
1 6-ounce can frozen orange juice concentrate
1/2 cup light corn syrup
1 cup semisweet chocolate chips
1 5-ounce can evaporated milk
1 1/2 cups miniature marshmallows

Sprinkle wafer crumbs in 8-inch square dish. Combine ice cream and orange juice concentrate in bowl. Spread in prepared dish. Freeze until firm. Combine corn syrup, chocolate chips, evaporated milk and marshmallows in double boiler. Cook over hot water until chocolate melts; mix well. Cool. Spread over frozen layer. Freeze until firm.

Yield: 6 servings.   **Prep Time:** 10 minutes plus freezing.

ORANGE SHERBET DESSERT

**1 6-ounce package orange gelatin
3 cups boiling water   1/2 cup milk
1 envelope whipped topping mix
1 pint orange sherbet, softened**

Dissolve gelatin in boiling water in bowl. Cool to room temperature. Combine milk with whipped topping mix in bowl. Prepare using package directions. Fold into gelatin mixture. Fold in sherbet. Spoon into 2-quart dish. Chill until set. May substitute desired flavors of gelatin and sherbet.

Yield: 12 servings.   **Prep Time:** 10 minutes plus chilling.

PEANUT-ICE CREAM DESSERT

**1/2 cup melted margarine
2 cups graham cracker crumbs   1/2 cup sugar
1 12-ounce can evaporated milk
1/2 cup margarine   2 cups confectioners' sugar
2/3 cup chocolate chips   1 teaspoon vanilla extract
1/2 gallon vanilla ice cream, softened
1/2 cup chopped salted peanuts
12 ounces whipped topping**

Combine 1/2 cup melted margarine, graham cracker crumbs and sugar in bowl; mix until crumbly. Reserve 1/2 cup crumb mixture. Press remaining crumb mixture into 9x13-inch baking dish. Bake at 350 degrees for 10 minutes or until light brown. Combine evaporated milk, remaining 1/2 cup margarine, confectioners' sugar, chocolate chips and vanilla in saucepan; mix well. Bring to a boil over medium heat, stirring constantly. Boil for 8 minutes, stirring constantly; remove from heat. Cool. Layer ice cream and chocolate mixture over baked layer. Sprinkle with peanuts. Spread with whipped topping; sprinkle with reserved crumb mixture. Freeze until firm.

Yield: 20 servings.   **Prep Time:** 25 minutes plus freezing.

PEANUT BUSTER PARFAIT

1½ cups sweetened condensed milk
2 cups confectioners' sugar
⅔ cup chocolate chips
½ cup butter or margarine
1   16-ounce package Oreo cookies, crushed
½ cup butter or margarine, softened
2 cups Spanish peanuts
½ gallon vanilla ice cream, softened

Combine condensed milk and confectioners' sugar in sauce-pan; mix well. Add chocolate chips and ½ cup butter. Simmer for 8 minutes, stirring constantly; cool. Combine cookie crumbs and remaining ½ cup butter in bowl; mix well. Press into 9x13-inch dish. Sprinkle with peanuts. Spread softened ice cream over cookie crust. Drizzle with chocolate mixture. Freeze until firm.

Yield: 16 servings.   **Prep Time:** 15 minutes plus freezing.

FROZEN PIÑA COLADA ICE CREAM DESSERT

1 quart vanilla ice cream, softened
1 cup cream of coconut
1   8-ounce can crushed pineapple, drained
½ cup chopped walnuts
1 cup shredded sweetened coconut, toasted

Beat ice cream, cream of coconut, pineapple and walnuts in mixer bowl. Pour into 9-inch springform pan. Freeze, covered, until firm. Remove side of springform pan. Sprinkle with toasted coconut.

Yield: 12 servings.   **Prep Time:** 5 minutes plus freezing.

PINEAPPLE-ORANGE PARFAITS

1   6-ounce can frozen orange juice concentrate, thawed
1/4 cup crushed pineapple
4 cups vanilla ice cream

Combine orange juice concentrate and pineapple in bowl; mix well. Alternate layers of ice cream and pineapple mixture in 8 parfait glasses. Freeze until serving time.

Yield: 8 servings.   **Prep Time:** 5 minutes plus freezing.

PUMPKIN ICE CREAM PIE

20 gingersnaps
1/4 cup melted margarine
1 cup solid-pack pumpkin
1 1/4 cups sugar
1 teaspoon cinnamon
1/2 teaspoon salt
1/2 teaspoon ginger
1 cup whipping cream, whipped
1 pint vanilla ice cream, softened
1 cup whipped cream

Crush gingersnaps, reserving 2 tablespoons. Combine crushed gingersnaps and margarine in bowl; mix well. Press into 9-inch freezerproof pie plate. Combine pumpkin, sugar, cinnamon, salt and ginger in bowl; mix well. Fold in 1 cup whipped cream and ice cream. Spread in prepared pie plate. Freeze until firm. Top with remaining 1 cup whipped cream. Garnish with reserved gingersnap crumbs.

Yield: 10 servings.   **Prep Time:** 15 minutes plus freezing.

RAINBOW ICE CREAM CAKE

1   10-ounce package frozen sliced
strawberries, partially thawed
Sugar to taste
1 angel food cake, cut into 1-inch pieces
1   3-ounce package lime-flavored gelatin
1   3-ounce package orange-flavored gelatin
1   3-ounce package strawberry-flavored gelatin
2 cups blueberries
1   15-ounce can mandarin oranges, drained
½ gallon vanilla ice cream, softened

Combine strawberries and sugar in bowl; mix well. Divide cake in 3 bowls. Stir 1 flavor of gelatin into each bowl; mix well. Layer strawberries, strawberry-flavored cake, blueberries, lime-flavored cake, oranges and orange-flavored cake in tube pan. placing ⅓ of the ice cream atop each layer of cake. Freeze until firm. Unmold onto serving plate.

Yield: 16 servings.   **Prep Time:** 20 minutes plus freezing.

STRAWBERRIES ROMANOFF

1 pint vanilla ice cream, softened
2 cups whipped cream
1 teaspoon rum extract
Juice of 1 lemon
2 quarts fresh whole strawberries

Fold softened ice cream and whipped cream together in bowl. Add rum extract and lemon juice; mix gently. Add strawberries; mix gently. Spoon into dessert bowls.

Yield: 6 servings.   **Prep Time:** 5 minutes.

*Whipped topping has fewer calories and less saturated
fat than whipped cream.*

GIANT ICE CREAM SUNDAE

3 cups graham cracker crumbs
1/2 cup melted margarine   3 bananas, sliced
1/2 gallon vanilla ice cream, sliced
1/2 cup salted peanuts
1/2 cup chocolate chips   1/4 cup margarine
1 cup confectioners' sugar
3/4 cup evaporated milk
1/2 teaspoon vanilla extract
16 ounces whipped topping

Combine cracker crumbs with 1/2 cup margarine in bowl; mix well. Press into 9x13-inch dish. Arrange banana slices in prepared dish. Layer ice cream slices over bananas. Sprinkle with peanuts. Place in freezer. Combine chocolate chips, 1/4 cup margarine, confectioners' sugar and evaporated milk in saucepan. Cook until thickened and smooth, stirring constantly. Stir in vanilla; cool. Spread over ice cream. Top with whipped topping. Freeze until serving time.

Yield: 15 servings.   **Prep Time:** 10 minutes plus freezing.

OREO SUNDAE DESSERT

1   16-ounce package Oreo cookies, crushed
1/2 cup melted margarine
1/2 gallon chocolate chip ice cream, softened
1 cup sugar   1/2 cup margarine
1 ounce unsweetened chocolate
1   12-ounce can evaporated milk
16 ounces whipped topping

Combine cookie crumbs and margarine in bowl; mix well. Pat into 9x13-inch dish. Freeze until firm. Spread ice cream over cookie layer. Freeze until firm. Combine sugar, 1/2 cup margarine, chocolate and evaporated milk in saucepan. Cook for 5 minutes. Cool. Pour over ice cream. Freeze until firm. Top with whipped topping. Freeze until serving time.

Yield: 16 servings.   **Prep Time:** 10 minutes plus freezing.

TERRIFIC ICE CREAM DESSERT

1   16-ounce package chocolate sandwich
cookies, crushed
³/₄ cup melted butter
¹/₂ gallon chocolate chip ice cream, softened
1¹/₂ cups chocolate syrup   ¹/₂ cup margarine
1   14-ounce can sweetened condensed milk
1 cup pecans

Combine cookie crumbs and ³/₄ cup melted butter in bowl; mix well. Press into 9x13-inch glass dish. Spread ice cream over cookie crust. Freeze until firm. Bring chocolate syrup, margarine and condensed milk to a boil in saucepan, stirring frequently. Cool to room temperature. Pour over ice cream layer; sprinkle with pecans. Freeze until serving time.

Yield: 16 servings.   **Prep Time:** 10 minutes plus freezing.

THANKSGIVING DESSERT

³/₄ cup graham cracker crumbs
¹/₄ cup sugar
¹/₄ cup melted margarine
1 cup pumpkin purée
1 pint vanilla ice cream, softened
¹/₂ teaspoon each ginger, cinnamon and nutmeg
Salt to taste

Mix cracker crumbs, sugar and margarine in bowl. Spread in 8x8-inch dish. Combine pumpkin, ice cream, ginger, cinnamon, nutmeg and salt in bowl; mix well. Spread mixture in prepared dish. Freeze until firm. May substitute frozen yogurt for ice cream.

Yield: 6 servings.   **Prep Time:** 10 minutes plus freezing.

Check ingredients on chocolate sandwich cookie package.
Some brands use saturated fat for filling.

FROZEN CHRISTMAS BOMBE

1/2 cup candied cherry halves   1/2 cup raisins
1/2 cup chopped candied pineapple   1/4 cup water
1 teaspoon rum extract   1/2 cup chopped pecans
1/3 cup chopped crystallized ginger
6 cups vanilla ice cream, softened
1 cup whipping cream   1/4 cup confectioners' sugar
1/2 teaspoon rum extract   Candied rose petals or violets

Bring first 4 ingredients to a boil in saucepan; remove from heat. Cool. Stir in 1 teaspoon rum extract. Sprinkle pecans on baking sheet. Bake at 350 degrees for 5 to 7 minutes or until golden brown. Cool. Add to fruit mixture with ginger; mix well. Line 8-cup mold with plastic wrap. Spoon 1 1/2 cups ice cream into prepared mold, pressing to 1-inch thickness. Layer fruit mixture and remaining ice cream 1/3 at a time in prepared mold. Freeze, covered, until firm. Beat whipping cream in mixer bowl until thickened. Chill, covered, until serving time. Unmold bombe onto serving plate; remove plastic wrap. Spread or pipe with whipped cream. Garnish with candied rose petals or violets.

Yield: 10 servings.   **Prep Time:** 25 minutes plus freezing.

WATERMELON BOMBE

1 pint lime sherbet, partially softened
1 pint pineapple sherbet, partially softened
1 pint raspberry sherbet, partially softened
1/4 cup semisweet chocolate chips

Line 1 1/2-quart bowl with 12x15-inch piece of foil. Spread lime sherbet over bottom and side of prepared bowl. Freeze until firm. Press and shape pineapple sherbet over lime sherbet layer. Freeze until firm. Pack raspberry sherbet into center, smoothing top to resemble cut watermelon. Freeze until firm. Unmold onto serving plate; remove foil. Cut into wedges. Press chocolate chips into wedges to resemble seeds. Serve immediately.

Yield: 8 servings.   **Prep Time:** 15 minutes plus freezing.

ICE CREAM SANDWICH DESSERT

4 8-ounce packages ice cream sandwiches
¾ cup coffee   ½ cup chocolate syrup
16 ounces whipped topping

Line 9x13-inch pan with ice cream sandwiches, cutting to fit. Prick with fork. Pour mixture of coffee and chocolate syrup over ice cream. Spread with whipped topping. Freeze, covered, until firm. Remove from freezer. Let stand for 15 minutes. Cut into slices.

Yield: 15 servings.   **Prep Time:** 10 minutes plus freezing.

BROILED PEACHES FLAMBÉ

8 peach halves   ½ cup packed light brown sugar
8 teaspoons margarine   8 scoops vanilla ice cream

Arrange peach halves cut side up in ovenproof dish. Place 1 tablespoon brown sugar and 1 teaspoon margarine in center of each. Broil until brown sugar melts and peaches are heated through. Serve with ice cream on serving dishes.

Yield: 8 servings.   **Prep Time:** 10 minutes.

VANILLA ORANGE DELIGHT

1 cup flour   ¼ cup packed dark brown sugar
½ cup melted margarine
½ gallon vanilla ice cream, softened
1 quart orange sherbet, softened   4 cups whipped topping

Combine flour, brown sugar and margarine in bowl; mix well. Spread in 9x13-inch baking dish. Bake at 350 degrees for 15 minutes, stirring 3 times. Reserve ⅓ cup crumbs. Cool remaining crumbs in dish. Layer vanilla ice cream, orange sherbet and whipped topping over cooled crumb crust; sprinkle with reserved crumbs. Freeze until serving time.

Yield: 12 servings.   **Prep Time:** 20 minutes plus freezing.

CHERRY-CHOCOLATE CHIP ICE CREAM

2 cups sugar
8 eggs, beaten
2   4-ounce packages vanilla instant pudding mix
1 quart half and half
1 tablespoon vanilla extract
1 cup maraschino cherries, chopped
1   16-ounce Hershey bar, shaved

Combine sugar, eggs, vanilla pudding mix, half and half and vanilla in mixer bowl; mix well. Pour into ice cream freezer container. Freeze using manufacturer's instructions until thickened. Add chopped cherries and shaved chocolate. Freeze until firm.

Yield: 18 servings.   **Prep Time:** 5 minutes plus freezing.

CHERRY MASH ICE CREAM

4 eggs
1½ cups sugar
2 cups whipping cream
1   14-ounce can sweetened condensed milk
2 tablespoons vanilla extract
1   12-ounce can evaporated milk
8 Cherry Mash candy bars
4 cups (about) milk

Beat eggs in large mixer bowl until foamy. Add sugar gradually, beating until thickened. Add whipping cream, condensed milk, vanilla and evaporated milk; mix well. Heat candy bars in saucepan until soft. Add to milk mixture; mix well. Pour into ice cream freezer container. Add whole milk to fill line. Freeze using manufacturer's instructions.

Yield: 20 servings.   **Prep Time:** 10 minutes plus freezing.

STRAWBERRY ICE CREAM

4 eggs, beaten   1½ cups sugar
1   14-ounce can sweetened condensed milk
1½ quarts milk   1½ teaspoons vanilla extract
4 cups mashed strawberries

Combine eggs and sugar in mixer bowl; beat until light and fluffy. Add condensed milk, milk, vanilla and strawberries; mix well. Pour into ice cream freezer container. Freeze using manufacturer's instructions.

Yield: 12 servings.   **Prep Time:** 5 minutes plus freezing.

OREO ICE CREAM

3 egg yolks
1   14-ounce can sweetened condensed milk
2 cups whipping cream, whipped
4 teaspoons vanilla extract
1 cup Oreo cookie crumbs

Beat egg yolks in large bowl. Stir in condensed milk and whipped cream. Add vanilla and crumbs; mix well. Spoon into 2-quart freezer container. Freeze, covered, until firm.

Yield: 8 servings.   **Prep Time:** 5 minutes plus freezing.

ELEGANT PEACHY BERRY SAUCE

2 tablespoons sugar
1½ tablespoons cornstarch
2 peaches, peeled, sliced   ½ cup red currant jelly
½ cup fresh blueberries   ½ cup fresh raspberries

Mix sugar and cornstarch in saucepan. Add peaches and jelly. Cook until thickened, stirring frequently. Stir in berries. Serve warm over ice cream.

Yield: 10 servings.   **Prep Time:** 10 minutes.

EXQUISITE CHOCOLATE SAUCE

¼ cup baking cocoa
¾ cup sugar   ⅓ cup light corn syrup
⅓ cup water
1 ounce unsweetened chocolate
3 tablespoons unsalted butter
¼ cup whipping cream   ⅛ teaspoon salt
1 teaspoon vanilla extract

Sift cocoa and sugar together. Cook corn syrup in saucepan until it forms thick threads when dropped from spoon. Stir in water. Add cocoa mixture; mix well. Cook until sugar dissolves, stirring frequently. Add chocolate. Cook until chocolate melts, stirring frequently. Blend in butter and whipping cream. Boil for 15 seconds. Remove from heat. Beat in salt and vanilla. Serve warm or cool. Store in tightly covered jar in refrigerator. Reheat to serve.

Yield: 10 servings.   **Prep Time:** 10 minutes.

HONEY-ORANGE CRANBERRY SAUCE

3 apples, peeled, finely chopped
Juice from 2 oranges
1 cinnamon stick
3 cups cranberries
Grated rind of 1 orange
⅔ cup honey
2 tablespoons frozen orange juice concentrate

Combine apples, orange juice and cinnamon stick in saucepan. Simmer over low heat for 10 minutes, stirring to mash apples. Add cranberries, orange rind and honey. Simmer over low heat for 10 to 15 minutes or until sauce thickens and cranberries pop, stirring occasionally. Cool. Remove cinnamon stick; stir in orange juice concentrate.

Yield: 15 servings.   **Prep Time:** 20 minutes.

Mexican Chocolate Sauce

3 ounces unsweetened baking chocolate
1/3 cup margarine
4 eggs
1 1/2 cups sugar
1 cup light corn syrup
1 1/2 teaspoons vanilla extract
1/8 teaspoon cinnamon
1 1/2 cups pecan halves

Combine chocolate and margarine in microwave-safe bowl. Microwave on High until melted. Combine eggs and sugar in mixer bowl; beat well. Add corn syrup, vanilla and cinnamon; mix well. Stir into chocolate mixture. Fold in pecans. Microwave on Medium-High for 5 minutes. Let stand for 5 minutes. Stir well. Microwave on Medium for 4 minutes. Serve warm on ice cream or white cake.

Yield: 20 servings.   **Prep Time:** 20 minutes.

Rich Caramel Sauce

1/2 cup sugar
1/2 cup packed light brown sugar
2 tablespoons all-purpose flour
1 cup whipping cream
1/4 cup margarine
2 teaspoons vanilla extract

Combine sugar, brown sugar, flour and whipping cream in saucepan. Bring to a boil, stirring frequently. Simmer for 3 minutes. Remove from heat. Beat in margarine and vanilla.

Yield: 10 servings.   **Prep Time:** 5 minutes.

Substitute evaporated skim milk for whipping cream in cooked sauces to greatly reduce calories and fat.

SIMPLY DELICIOUS CAKES

Nutritional information for Simply Delicious Cakes is on pages 155–156.

APRICOT ANGEL CAKE

1⅓ cups sugar
7 tablespoons cornstarch
1   46-ounce can apricot nectar
1 prepared angel food cake
16 ounces whipped topping
⅓ cup pecans

Combine sugar, cornstarch and apricot nectar in saucepan; mix well. Cook over medium heat until transparent, stirring constantly; cool. Tear angel food cake into bite-sized pieces. Layer cake and apricot mixture in tube pan. Chill until firm. Unmold onto cake plate. Spread whipped topping over top. Sprinkle with pecans. Chill, covered, until serving time.

Yield: 15 servings.   **Prep Time:** 10 minutes plus chilling.

APPLE DOWNSIDE-UP CAKE

2 tablespoons margarine
¼ cup packed brown sugar
2 medium apples, sliced
2 cups baking mix
2 tablespoons sugar
1 teaspoon cinnamon
¼ teaspoon nutmeg
1 egg
⅔ cup water

Melt margarine in 9-inch cake pan. Sprinkle with brown sugar. Arrange apples over brown sugar. Combine baking mix, sugar, cinnamon, nutmeg, egg and water in mixer bowl. Beat for 30 seconds. Spoon evenly over apples. Bake at 400 degrees for 25 to 30 minutes or until cake tests done. Invert onto heatproof serving plate. Serve with whipped cream.

Yield: 8 servings.   **Prep Time:** 10 minutes plus baking.

GRANNY'S APPLESAUCE CAKE

1 cup raisins, chopped
1½ cups flour
1 teaspoon cinnamon
½ teaspoon cloves
1 teaspoon salt
½ cup butter, softened
1 cup sugar
1 teaspoon baking soda
1 cup unsweetened applesauce

Combine raisins and flour in bowl. Add spices and salt; mix well. Cream butter and sugar in mixer bowl until light and fluffy. Add raisin mixture; mix well. Mix baking soda into applesauce in bowl. Fold into batter mixture. Pour into 9x9-inch cake pan. Bake at 350 degrees for 30 minutes or until cake tests done.

Yield: 9 servings.　　　**Prep Time:** 10 minutes plus baking.

EASY BANANA CAKE

1 medium banana, mashed
2 envelopes instant hot chocolate mix
2 packets artificial sweetener
2 tablespoons flour
1 teaspoon baking powder
Cinnamon to taste
1 teaspoon vanilla extract

Combine banana, chocolate drink mix, sweetener, flour, baking powder, cinnamon and vanilla in bowl; mix well. Spoon into miniature loaf pan sprayed with nonstick cooking spray. Bake at 350 degrees for 15 minutes. Remove to wire rack to cool.

Yield: 2 servings.　　　**Prep Time:** 5 minutes plus baking.

BLUEBERRY TEA CAKE

4 cups flour   1 tablespoon baking powder
½ teaspoon salt
1 cup butter, softened   1¼ cups sugar
2 eggs   1 cup milk
4 cups fresh blueberries
1 cup sugar   ½ cup flour
2 teaspoons cinnamon   ½ cup butter

Mix 4 cups flour, baking powder and salt in bowl. Cream 1 cup butter and 1¼ cups sugar in mixer bowl until light and fluffy. Beat in eggs and milk. Add flour mixture gradually, mixing well after each addition. Fold in blueberries; batter will be stiff. Spoon into greased and floured 9x13-inch cake pan. Mix 1 cup sugar, ½ cup flour and cinnamon in bowl. Cut in ½ cup butter until crumbly. Sprinkle over batter. Bake at 300 degrees for 30 minutes or until cake tests done. Cool on wire rack.

Yield: 12 servings.   **Prep Time:** 10 minutes plus baking.

BROWN SUGAR CAKE

¾ cup melted margarine
1   1-pound package light brown sugar
3 eggs
1 tablespoon vanilla extract
1 cup coconut
1 cup chopped pecans
2½ cups flour

Combine margarine, brown sugar, eggs, vanilla, coconut and pecans in mixer bowl; mix well. Add flour; mix well. Spoon into greased and floured 9x12-inch cake pan. Bake at 350 degrees for 30 minutes or until cake tests done.

Yield: 15 servings.   **Prep Time:** 10 minutes plus baking.

MICROWAVE CARROT CAKE

1 cup oil   1 cup grated carrots
1 cup sugar   2 eggs
1/2 cup orange juice
1 teaspoon vanilla extract
1 3/4 cups sifted flour
1 teaspoon baking powder
1 teaspoon baking soda
1/2 teaspoon each cinnamon, nutmeg and salt
1/2 cup raisins

Combine oil and carrots in blender container. Process for 30 seconds. Add sugar, eggs, orange juice and vanilla. Process for 10 to 15 seconds. Stir into sifted dry ingredients in bowl; mix well. Stir in raisins. Pour into ungreased microwave-safe tube pan. Microwave on Medium for 10 minutes, turning pan 1/4 turn every 3 minutes. Microwave on High for 3 minutes or until cake tests done. Cool in pan for 10 minutes. Invert onto cake plate to cool completely. May frost with cream cheese frosting.

Yield: 16 servings.   **Prep Time:** 10 minutes plus cooking.

CHOCOLATE CHIP CAKE

1   4-ounce package chocolate pudding and pie filling mix
2 1/2 cups milk
1   2-layer package dark chocolate cake mix
1 cup chocolate chips
1 cup chopped pecans

Combine pudding mix and milk in saucepan; mix well. Cook using package directions. Add cake mix gradually, stirring constantly. Batter will be very stiff. Spread evenly in greased and floured 10x15-inch cake pan. Sprinkle chocolate chips and pecans over top; press lightly into batter. Bake at 350 degrees for 30 minutes or until cake tests done. Cool in pan.

Yield: 24 servings.   **Prep Time:** 10 minutes plus baking.

CHOCOLATE CHEESE CUPCAKES

1   2-layer package devil's food cake mix
1 egg
8 ounces cream cheese, softened
¾ cup sugar
¾ cup chocolate chips

Prepare cake mix using package directions. Fill paper-lined muffin cups ⅔ full. Combine egg, cream cheese and sugar in mixer bowl; mix well. Stir in chocolate chips. Drop 1 teaspoonful into each muffin cup. Bake using package directions or until cupcakes test done. Remove to wire rack to cool.

Yield: 24 servings.   **Prep Time:** 10 minutes plus baking.

MEXICAN CHOCOLATE CAKE

1   2-layer package chocolate cake mix
1½ to 2 teaspoons cinnamon
½ cup margarine
2 ounces baking chocolate
6 tablespoons milk
1   1-pound package confectioners' sugar, sifted
1 teaspoon vanilla extract
1 to 1½ cups chopped pecans

Prepare cake mix using package directions, adding cinnamon. Pour into greased and floured 9x13-inch cake pan. Bake at 350 degrees for 20 minutes or until cake tests done. Heat margarine, baking chocolate and milk in saucepan until bubbles form around edge of saucepan; remove from heat. Add confectioners' sugar, vanilla and pecans; mix well. Spread over warm cake.

Yield: 15 servings.   **Prep Time:** 10 minutes plus baking.

CHOCOLATE CHERRY CAKE

1 2-layer package chocolate cake mix
2 eggs, beaten
1 21-ounce can cherry pie filling
1 teaspoon almond extract

Combine cake mix, eggs, pie filling and almond extract in mixer bowl; mix well. Pour into greased and floured 9x13-inch cake pan. Bake at 350 degrees for 30 minutes or until cake tests done. Cool in pan.

Yield: 15 servings.   **Prep Time:** 5 minutes plus baking.

CHOCOLATE SUNDAE CAKE

1 2-layer package devil's food cake mix
1 18-ounce jar hot fudge sauce, warmed
1 18-ounce jar caramel sauce, warmed
12 ounces whipped topping
1 cup chopped pecans

Prepare cake mix using package directions. Pour into greased 9x13-inch cake pan. Bake at 350 degrees for 35 minutes. Make deep indentations in hot cake using end of wooden spoon. Layer hot fudge sauce and caramel sauce over top of cake. Chill until serving time. Spread with whipped topping; sprinkle with pecans. Cut into squares.

Yield: 20 servings.   **Prep Time:** 10 minutes plus baking.

*New lite cake mixes and pie fillings reduce calories
and fat but not flavor!*

WACKY CHOCOLATE CAKE

1½ cups flour
1 cup sugar
3 tablespoons baking cocoa
½ teaspoon salt
1 teaspoon baking soda
1 tablespoon vinegar
6 tablespoons oil
1 teaspoon vanilla extract

Mix flour, sugar, cocoa, salt and baking soda in 8x8-inch cake pan. Make 3 wells in mixture with spoon. Pour vinegar into 1 well, oil into 1 well and vanilla into 1 well. Pour water over all. Stir with fork until well mixed. Bake at 350 degrees for 25 minutes or until toothpick inserted in center comes out clean.

Yield: 9 servings.   **Prep Time:** 10 minutes plus baking.

COCONUT CAKE

1 baked 9x13-inch white cake
1 14-ounce can sweetened condensed milk
1 8-ounce can cream of coconut
8 ounces whipped topping
2 cups shredded coconut

Make deep indentations in hot cake using wooden dowel. Combine condensed milk and cream of coconut in bowl; mix well. Pour over warm cake. Let stand until cooled completely. Spread whipped topping over top of cake; sprinkle with coconut. Store in refrigerator.

Yield: 16 servings.   **Prep Time:** 10 minutes plus cooling.

*If you must use disposable plates and cups for a party
or picnic, buy recyclable paper instead of plastic or foam.*

CRANBERRY CUPCAKES

1/2 cup melted margarine
1/3 cup shortening
1 1/2 cups sugar
4 eggs   2 1/2 cups flour
1 teaspoon cinnamon
1/2 teaspoon baking powder
1   16-ounce can cranberry sauce
1 1/2 cups applesauce

Cream margarine, shortening and sugar in mixer bowl until light and fluffy. Add eggs 1 at a time, beating well after each addition. Add flour, cinnamon, baking powder, cranberry sauce and applesauce; mix well. Fill 12 paper-lined muffin cups 2/3 full. Bake at 350 degrees for 30 minutes or until cupcakes test done. Remove to wire rack to cool.

Yield: 12 servings.   **Prep Time:** 10 minutes plus baking.

FRUITCAKE CUPCAKES

8 ounces candied cherries, chopped
1 pound dates, chopped
8 ounces candied pineapple, chopped
1   4-ounce package coconut
2 cups chopped pecans
1/4 teaspoon salt
1/2 teaspoon vanilla extract
1   14-ounce can sweetened condensed milk

Combine cherries, dates, pineapple, coconut and pecans in bowl; mix well. Mix salt, vanilla and condensed milk together in bowl. Add to fruit; mix well. Fill miniature muffin cups 2/3 full. Bake at 325 degrees for 25 to 30 minutes or until cupcakes test done. Cool in pan for several minutes. Invert onto wire rack to cool completely. Store in tightly covered container for 2 weeks before serving.

Yield: 35 servings.   **Prep Time:** 15 minutes plus baking.

NO-BAKE FRUITCAKE

1 16-ounce package graham crackers, crushed
1 8-ounce jar maraschino cherries, chopped
1 cup chopped orange slice candy
1 cup chopped pecans
1/2 cup coconut
1 cup chopped raisins
1 10-ounce package miniature marshmallows
1/2 cup butter   1/4 cup milk

Combine graham cracker crumbs, cherries, candy, pecans, coconut and raisins in bowl; mix well. Melt marshmallows with butter and milk in double boiler, stirring to mix well. Add to fruit mixture; mix well. Pack into round cake pan. Garnish as desired.

Yield: 20 servings.   **Prep Time:** 15 minutes.

HARVEST SNACK CAKE

1/2 cup margarine
1 small jar baby food sweet potatoes
1 cup crushed pineapple
1 egg
1 cup sugar
1 teaspoon baking soda
1/2 teaspoon salt
1 1/4 cups flour
1 teaspoon vanilla extract
2 teaspoons cinnamon
1 cup chopped pecans

Melt margarine in 8x8-inch cake pan. Add sweet potatoes, pineapple, egg, sugar, baking soda, salt, flour, vanilla, cinnamon and pecans; mix well with fork. Bake at 325 degrees for 30 minutes or until cake tests done. Serve warm or cold.

Yield: 9 servings.   **Prep Time:** 10 minutes plus baking.

HURRY-UP CAKES

2 cups sifted cake flour
2 teaspoons baking powder
1¼ cups sugar
½ cup shortening
¾ cup milk
1 teaspoon vanilla extract
2 eggs

Mix flour, baking powder and sugar in mixer bowl. Add shortening, milk, vanilla and eggs; mix well. Spoon into 2 greased and floured 9-inch cake pans. Bake at 375 degrees for 30 minutes. Remove to wire rack to cool. May frost if desired.

Yield: 12 servings.   **Prep Time:** 10 minutes plus baking.

ICE CREAM CONE CUPCAKES

1 2-layer package yellow cake mix
36 flat-bottomed ice cream cones
2 egg whites
¼ teaspoon salt
¼ cup sugar
¾ cup light corn syrup
1¼ teaspoons vanilla extract
Red food coloring

Prepare cake mix using package directions. Stand ice cream cones in muffin cups. Place 1 tablespoon cake batter in each cone. Bake at 350 degrees for 15 to 20 minutes or until brown. Beat egg whites in mixer bowl until soft peaks form. Add salt and sugar gradually, beating until smooth and glossy. Add corn syrup in slow steady stream, beating until stiff peaks form. Fold in vanilla and red food coloring. Swirl generously over cupcakes.

Yield: 36 servings.   **Prep Time:** 10 minutes plus baking.

LEMON ANGEL ROLL

1 package 1-step angel food cake mix
1 21-ounce can lemon pie filling
1/2 cup confectioners' sugar
8 ounces cream cheese, softened
1/2 cup margarine, softened   4 cups confectioners' sugar
1 teaspoon vanilla extract   1 cup confectioners' sugar
1 to 2 tablespoons lemon juice

Combine cake mix and pie filling in mixer bowl. Beat until well blended. Spread in ungreased 10x15-inch cake pan. Bake at 350 degrees for 20 to 25 minutes or until cake tests done. Invert onto towel sprinkled with 1/2 cup confectioners' sugar. Roll up cake in towel. Cool. Beat cream cheese and margarine in mixer bowl until light and fluffy. Add 4 cups confectioners' sugar and vanilla; beat until smooth. Unroll cake. Spread with cream cheese mixture. Roll as for jelly roll. Place on serving plate. Mix 1 cup confectioners' sugar with enough lemon juice to make of glaze consistency. Drizzle over cake roll.

Yield: 16 servings.   **Prep Time:** 10 minutes plus baking.

LEMON CHIFFON CAKE

5 egg whites, at room temperature
2 tablespoons sifted confectioners' sugar
1 1/2 cups sifted cake flour   1 cup sugar
2 teaspoons baking powder
1/4 teaspoon salt   1/2 cup oil
Grated rind of 2 lemons   1/2 cup fresh lemon juice

Beat egg whites with confectioners' sugar in large mixer bowl just until stiff peaks form. Sift flour, sugar, baking powder and salt into medium mixer bowl. Make well in center. Add oil, lemon rind and juice. Beat at medium speed until smooth. Fold gently into egg whites. Spoon into ungreased 9-inch tube pan. Bake at 350 degrees for 30 minutes or until golden brown. Cool in pan for 5 minutes. Invert onto wire rack to cool completely.

Yield: 16 servings.   **Prep Time:** 15 minutes plus baking.

Mocha Pound Cake

1 pound cake
6 Heath candy bars
8 ounces whipped topping
1 teaspoon instant coffee

Slice cake horizontally into 3 layers. Place on serving plate. Chop candy into fine pieces, reserving 2 tablespoons. Fold remaining candy into whipped topping. Stir in coffee powder. Spread between layers and over top and side of cake. Sprinkle with reserved candy.

Yield: 8 servings.   **Prep Time:** 10 minutes.

Orange Cake

½ cup margarine   4 eggs
1   11-ounce can mandarin oranges
1   2-layer package yellow cake mix
12 ounces whipped topping
1   4-ounce package vanilla instant pudding mix
1   16-ounce can crushed pineapple, drained

Cream margarine in mixer bowl until light and fluffy. Add eggs 1 at a time, beating well after each addition. Add mandarin oranges and juice; beat well. Add cake mix; mix well. Pour into 2 greased and floured cake pans. Bake at 350 degrees for 25 to 30 minutes or until cake tests done. Cool in pans for several minutes. Invert onto wire rack to cool completely. Combine whipped topping and pudding mix in bowl; mix well. Add crushed pineapple; mix well. Spread between layers and over top and side of cooled cake.

Yield: 12 servings.   **Prep Time:** 15 minutes plus baking.

Shop at farmers' markets and co-ops for fresh produce which has not been pre-packaged.

OLD-FASHIONED CUPCAKES

²/₃ cup margarine, softened
2 cups sugar
4 eggs, beaten
1 cup milk
3¹/₄ cups flour
4 teaspoons baking powder
¹/₄ teaspoon mace

Cream margarine and sugar in mixer bowl until light and fluffy. Add eggs and milk; mix well. Sift flour, baking powder and mace together. Add to batter; mix well. Fill paper-lined muffin cups ³/₄ full. Bake at 350 degrees for 15 to 18 minutes or until cupcakes test done. Remove to wire rack to cool.

Yield: 30 servings.   **Prep Time:** 10 minutes plus baking.

PEANUT BUTTER CUPCAKES

1¹/₄ cups flour
1 cup packed brown sugar
³/₄ cup milk
¹/₄ cup peanut butter
1 egg
1 tablespoon margarine, softened
1 teaspoon vanilla extract
1¹/₂ teaspoons baking powder
¹/₂ teaspoon salt
¹/₂ cup semisweet chocolate chips

Combine flour, brown sugar, milk, peanut butter, egg, margarine, vanilla, baking powder, salt and chocolate chips in blender container. Process on high for 45 seconds, scraping down sides twice. Fill paper-lined muffin cups ²/₃ full. Bake at 350 degrees for 25 minutes or until cupcakes test done. Remove to wire rack to cool. May spread with peanut butter and sprinkle with peanuts.

Yield: 18 servings.   **Prep Time:** 10 minutes plus baking.

PEACH PRESERVE CAKE

1 cup margarine
2 cups sugar
4 eggs
3 cups flour
1 teaspoon cinnamon
1/3 teaspoon cloves
1 teaspoon baking soda
1 cup buttermilk
1 cup chopped pecans
1 cup peach preserves

Cream margarine and sugar in mixer bowl. Beat in eggs 1 at a time. Sift flour with cinnamon and cloves. Dissolve baking soda in buttermilk in bowl. Add alternately with flour mixture to creamed mixture. Stir in pecans and preserves. Pour into greased 9x13-inch cake pan. Bake at 350 degrees for 1 hour.

Yield: 15 servings.   **Prep Time:** 5 minutes plus baking.

SOUR CREAM PEACH CAKE

1   2-layer package orange cake mix
1   21-ounce can peach pie filling
1/2 cup sour cream
2 eggs

Combine cake mix, peach pie filling, sour cream and eggs in ungreased 10x15-inch cake pan. Mix with fork until well blended. Scrape sides and corners of pan with rubber spatula, spreading batter evenly. Bake at 350 degrees for 25 to 30 minutes. Store, loosely covered, in refrigerator.

Yield: 20 servings.   **Prep Time:** 5 minutes plus baking.

Pear Cake

1½ cups margarine, softened
2½ cups sugar   4 eggs
3 cups flour   1 teaspoon baking soda
1 teaspoon allspice   1 teaspoon nutmeg
1 teaspoon cinnamon
½ teaspoon salt   1 cup buttermilk
1 cup chopped pecans
1 cup pear preserves

Cream margarine and sugar in mixer bowl until light and fluffy. Beat in eggs 1 at a time. Mix flour, baking soda, spices and salt together. Add buttermilk and flour mixture alternately to creamed mixture, beating well. Stir in pecans and pear preserves. Pour into greased bundt pan. Bake at 325 degrees for 25 minutes or until cake tests done. May substitute other flavor preserves for pear.

Yield: 16 servings.   **Prep Time:** 10 minutes plus baking.

Microwave Pistachio Cake

1 cup finely chopped pecans
¾ cup sugar   2 tablespoons cinnamon
1   2-layer package yellow cake mix
1   4-ounce package instant pistachio pudding mix
4 eggs   1 cup sour cream
¾ cup orange juice   ¼ cup oil
1 teaspoon vanilla extract

Mix pecans, sugar and cinnamon in small bowl. Sprinkle ⅓ of the mixture into greased glass bundt pan. Combine cake mix, pudding mix, eggs, sour cream, orange juice, oil and vanilla in large bowl; mix well. Alternate layers of batter and cinnamon mixture in bundt pan. Swirl with fork. Microwave on High for 10 to 12 minutes or until cake tests done, rotating once. Let stand for 10 minutes.

Yield: 16 servings.   **Prep Time:** 10 minutes plus cooking.

PRALINE CAKE

1   2-layer package yellow cake mix
1/2 cup sugar   1/2 cup vegetable oil
1 cup milk   3 eggs
1/2 cup margarine, softened   2 eggs
1   1-pound package light brown sugar
2 tablespoons flour   1 teaspoon vanilla extract
11/2 cups coarsely chopped pecans

Combine cake mix, sugar, oil and milk in mixer bowl; mix well. Add 3 eggs 1 at a time, beating well after each addition. Pour into oiled 8x12-inch cake pan. Combine margarine, remaining 2 eggs, brown sugar and flour in mixer bowl; beat well. Stir in vanilla and pecans. Spread over top of batter. Bake at 350 degrees for 30 minutes.

Yield: 16 servings.   **Prep Time:** 10 minutes plus baking.

PUMPKIN CAKE ROLL

3 eggs   1 cup sugar
2/3 cup pumpkin pie filling   1 teaspoon lemon juice
3/4 teaspoon baking powder   2 teaspoons cinnamon
1 teaspoon ginger   3/4 cup flour
1/2 teaspoon nutmeg   1/2 teaspoon salt
1 cup chopped pecans   1 cup confectioners' sugar
6 ounces cream cheese, softened   1/4 cup butter, softened
1/2 teaspoon vanilla extract

Beat eggs in mixer bowl at high speed for 5 minutes. Beat in 1 cup sugar gradually. Stir in pie filling and lemon juice. Add baking powder, cinnamon, ginger, flour, nutmeg and salt; mix well. Spread in greased and floured 10x15-inch cake pan. Top with pecans. Bake at 375 degrees for 15 minutes. Invert onto towel sprinkled with confectioners' sugar. Roll cake in towel from narrow end. Cool on wire rack. Cream remaining ingredients in bowl until light and fluffy. Unroll cake. Spread with filling; reroll. Chill in refrigerator.

Yield: 12 servings.   **Prep Time:** 15 minutes plus baking.

RASPBERRY JELLY ROLL

3 eggs   ¼ cup milk
1 cup sugar   1 cup flour
1 teaspoon baking powder
⅛ teaspoon salt
¾ cup confectioners' sugar
1 cup raspberry preserves

Beat eggs in mixer bowl until thick and lemon-colored. Add milk; mix well. Add sugar, flour, baking powder and salt; mix well. Grease bottom of jelly roll pan; line with waxed paper. Spread batter onto prepared pan. Bake at 350 degrees for 15 minutes or until cake tests done. Invert onto towel sprinkled with confectioners' sugar; remove waxed paper. Roll in towel from narrow end. Cool seam side down on wire rack for 20 minutes. Unroll cake; remove towel. Spread with preserves; reroll. Place on serving plate. Sprinkle with remaining confectioners' sugar.

Yield: 12 servings.   **Prep Time:** 10 minutes plus baking.

SPONGE CAKE

1 cup milk   ½ cup butter
4 eggs   2 cups sugar
1 teaspoon vanilla extract
2 cups flour
2 teaspoons baking powder
1 teaspoon salt

Heat milk and butter in saucepan until butter melts; set aside. Beat eggs in mixer bowl until thick and lemon-colored. Add sugar ⅓ cup at a time, beating constantly. Add vanilla. Fold in sifted mixture of flour, baking powder and salt. Stir in warm milk. Spoon into greased 9x13-inch cake pan. Bake at 350 degrees for 30 minutes or until cake tests done.

Yield: 15 servings.   **Prep Time:** 10 minutes plus baking.

STRAWBERRY CAKE

1 2-layer package yellow cake mix
1 3-ounce package strawberry gelatin
1/2 cup water
1 cup oil
4 eggs
2 10-ounce packages frozen strawberries, thawed
2 tablespoons (or less) sugar
12 ounces whipped topping

Combine cake mix, gelatin, water, oil, eggs and 1 package strawberries in mixer bowl; mix until smooth. Spoon into greased 9x13-inch cake pan. Bake at 350 degrees for 30 minutes or until cake tests done. Cool on wire rack. Sweeten remaining package strawberries with sugar in bowl. Fold in whipped topping. Spread over cake.

Yield: 15 servings.   **Prep Time:** 10 minutes plus baking.

SUNSET CAKE

1 2-layer package yellow cake mix
3 eggs
1 cup vegetable oil
1 cup water
1 4-ounce package butterscotch instant pudding mix

Combine cake mix, eggs, oil, water and pudding mix in mixer bowl. Beat at low speed until moistened. Beat at medium speed for 4 minutes. Pour into greased and floured bundt pan. Bake at 350 degrees for 30 minutes or until cake tests done. May drizzle with orange glaze.

Yield: 12 servings.   **Prep Time:** 10 minutes plus baking.

*Use sour half and half for sour cream to
reduce calories and fat.*

WALNUT MOCHA CAKE

1 16-ounce package brownie mix
2 eggs
¼ cup water
½ cup coarsely chopped walnuts
2 cups whipping cream
½ cup packed light brown sugar
2 tablespoons instant coffee

Prepare brownie mix using package directions. Stir in eggs, water and chopped walnuts. Spoon batter into 2 greased and floured 9-inch cake pans. Bake at 350 degrees for 20 minutes. Cool in pans for several minutes. Invert onto wire rack to cool completely. Whip cream in mixer bowl just until thickened. Add brown sugar and instant coffee. Whip until soft peaks form. Spread between layers and over top and side of cooled cake. Garnish with walnut halves. Chill until serving time.

Yield: 12 servings.   **Prep Time:** 10 minutes plus baking.

WHITE GRAPE JUICE CAKE

1 2-layer package butter brickle cake mix
1 4-ounce package vanilla instant pudding mix
¾ cup vegetable oil
4 eggs
¾ cup white grape juice
1 cup confectioners' sugar

Combine cake mix and pudding mix in mixer bowl; mix well. Add oil and eggs; beat well. Pour into greased and floured bundt pan. Bake at 350 degrees for 25 minutes or until cake tests done. Cool in pan for several minutes. Invert onto serving plate. Combine white grape juice and confectioners' sugar in bowl; mix well. Pour over warm cake.

Yield: 16 servings.   **Prep Time:** 10 minutes plus baking.

LUSCIOUS SWEET TREATS

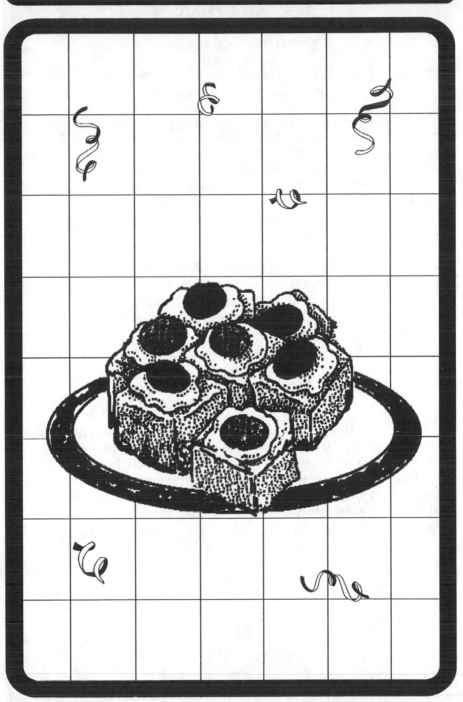

Nutritional information for Luscious Sweet Treats is on pages 156–157.

ALMOND CLUSTERS

2 tablespoons margarine
¼ cup milk
1 18-ounce package creamy frosting mix
1½ cups slivered almonds

Melt margarine with milk in saucepan over low heat; remove from heat. Stir in frosting mix. Cook over low heat for 1 to 2 minutes or until smooth and glossy, stirring constantly. Stir in slivered almonds. Drop by teaspoonfuls onto waxed paper. Let stand until firm. Add 2 additional teaspoons milk if using chocolate fudge frosting mix.

Yield: 24 servings.   **Prep Time:** 5 minutes plus standing.

SWEET AND SPICY ALMONDS

3 tablespoons vegetable oil
2 cups whole blanched almonds
½ cup sugar
1½ teaspoons salt
1½ teaspoons cumin
¼ to 1 teaspoon cayenne pepper
1 tablespoon sugar

Heat oil in skillet. Stir in almonds and ½ cup sugar. Cook for 10 minutes or until almonds are golden brown, stirring frequently. Pour into bowl. Sprinkle with mixture of salt, cumin, cayenne pepper and 1 tablespoon sugar; toss to coat. Spread in single layer on waxed paper-lined surface. Let stand until cool. Store in airtight container.

Yield: 16 servings.   **Prep Time:** 10 minutes plus standing.

BABY RUTH CANDY

2 cups semisweet chocolate chips
½ cup chunky peanut butter
1 7-ounce jar marshmallow creme
1 cup chopped salted peanuts

Melt chocolate chips and peanut butter in double boiler over hot water, stirring occasionally. Remove from heat. Add marshmallow creme and peanuts; beat until well mixed. Pour mixture into foil-lined 8x8-inch glass dish. Cool completely. Cut into squares.

Yield: 36 servings.   **Prep Time:** 10 minutes plus standing.

BAVARIAN MINTS

2 ounces unsweetened baking chocolate
2 cups semisweet chocolate chips
1 tablespoon butter
1 cup sweetened condensed milk
1 teaspoon peppermint extract

Melt unsweetened chocolate and chocolate chips in double boiler; mix well. Add butter, condensed milk and flavoring. Beat until smooth and creamy. Drop by spoonfuls onto waxed paper. Chill in refrigerator until firm. May substitute vanilla or other flavoring for peppermint if preferred. Do not use oil of peppermint for peppermint extract.

Yield: 24 servings.   **Prep Time:** 5 minutes plus chilling.

BUTTERSCOTCH CONFETTI

¼ cup margarine
½ cup peanut butter
1 cup butterscotch chips
1   8-ounce package miniature colored marshmallows
½ cup flaked coconut

Combine margarine, peanut butter and butterscotch chips in saucepan over low heat, stirring constantly. Let stand until cooled to lukewarm. Stir in marshmallows and coconut. Pour into 9-inch square pan lined with waxed paper. Chill until firm. Cut into squares.

Yield: 81 servings.   **Prep Time:** 5 minutes plus cooling.

CARAMEL FONDUE

1   16-ounce package caramels
8 ounces cream cheese
Fresh fruit wedges

Melt caramels and cream cheese together in double boiler, stirring frequently. Pour into heated fondue pot. Serve with fresh fruit wedges.

Yield: 24 servings.   **Prep Time:** 10 minutes.

*Neufchâtel or lite cream cheese "lighten up" recipes
using cream cheese. Used as a spread, cream
cheeses are lower in fat than butter.*

MICROWAVE CARAMELS

1 cup margarine, melted
1   1-pound package light brown sugar
1   14-ounce can sweetened condensed milk
1 cup light corn syrup
1 teaspoon vanilla extract
2 cups semisweet chocolate chips, melted

Blend margarine, brown sugar, condensed milk and corn syrup in large microwave-safe bowl. Microwave on High for 17 to 18 minutes, stirring every 3 minutes. Mix in vanilla. Pour into buttered 9x13-inch pan. Chill in refrigerator overnight. Pour melted chocolate over caramels. Cut into 1-inch squares. May substitute almond bark for chocolate chips or increase amount of chocolate and dip caramel squares into chocolate to coat on all sides.

Yield: 120 servings.   **Prep Time:** 20 minutes plus chilling.

CHOCOLATE CHIP BONBONS

3 ounces cream cheese, softened
2¼ cups confectioners' sugar
1 tablespoon melted butter or margarine
1 teaspoon vanilla extract
½ cup semisweet miniature chocolate chips
1 cup finely chopped pecans

Combine cream cheese, confectioners' sugar, butter and vanilla in bowl; blend well. Stir in chocolate chips. Chill for several minutes. Shape into ½-inch balls; coat with pecans. Chill until serving time. Serve cold.

Yield: 24 servings.   **Prep Time:** 5 minutes plus chilling.

CHOCOLATE AND PEANUT DROPS

2 cups milk chocolate chips
2 teaspoons shortening
2 cups unsalted peanuts

Melt chocolate chips and shortening in double boiler over hot water, stirring occasionally. Add peanuts; stir until coated with chocolate. Drop by spoonfuls onto greased waxed paper. Chill until firm. Store in cool place.

Yield: 30 servings.   **Prep Time:** 10 minutes plus chilling.

CHERRY BINGS

2 cups sugar
$2/3$ cup evaporated milk
12 large marshmallows
$1/2$ cup margarine
1 cup cherry baking chips
1 teaspoon vanilla extract
2 cups semisweet chocolate chips
$3/4$ cup peanut butter
1 tablespoon margarine
10 ounces salted peanuts, crushed

Bring sugar, evaporated milk, marshmallows and $1/2$ cup margarine to a boil in saucepan over medium heat, stirring constantly. Cook for 5 minutes; remove from heat. Stir in cherry chips and vanilla. Pour into buttered 9x13-inch dish. Melt chocolate chips in double boiler. Add peanut butter, 1 tablespoon margarine and peanuts; mix well. Spread over cherry layer. Chill until firm. Cut into small squares. May substitute chopped candied cherries for cherry chips if preferred.

Yield: 96 servings.   Prep Time: 15 minutes plus chilling.

CHERRY CANDY

1   14-ounce package chocolate frosting mix
1   1-pound package confectioners' sugar
1/2   14-ounce can sweetened condensed milk
1 1/2 teaspoons vanilla extract
1   4-ounce jar maraschino cherries, drained, chopped
1/4 cup margarine, softened
2 cups white chocolate chips
1 to 2 tablespoons melted paraffin
1   8-ounce jar salted peanuts, chopped

Combine dry frosting mix, confectioners' sugar, condensed milk, vanilla, cherries and margarine in bowl; mix well. Shape into balls. Chill until firm if necessary. Melt white chocolate chips with paraffin in double boiler over hot water; blend well. Dip balls into melted white chocolate; roll in peanuts to coat. Place in paper bonbon cups. Let stand until firm. Store in refrigerator.

Yield: 36 servings.   **Prep Time:** 20 minutes plus chilling.

COCONUT LEMON CLUSTERS

1   3-ounce package lemon pudding and pie filling mix
1 cup sugar
1/2 cup evaporated milk
1 tablespoon margarine, softened
1 cup flaked coconut

Mix dry pudding mix and sugar in saucepan. Add evaporated milk and margarine; mix well. Cook over medium heat until mixture comes to a boil, stirring constantly. Simmer for 3 minutes; remove from heat. Beat in coconut. Drop by spoonfuls onto waxed paper. May beat in several drops of hot water if necessary. Let stand until firm; place in paper bonbon cups.

Yield: 24 servings.   **Prep Time:** 10 minutes plus standing.

COFFEE CREAMS

1/2 cup margarine
1 tablespoon cream
1 1/2 teaspoons instant coffee granules
1 teaspoon vanilla extract
3 cups confectioners' sugar
1 egg white, stiffly beaten

Melt margarine with cream in double boiler over hot water; mix well. Add coffee granules and vanilla, stirring until coffee is completely dissolved. Sift in confectioners' sugar gradually, mixing well; mixture will be very stiff. Remove from heat. Add egg white; beat until smooth. Drop by small spoonfuls onto waxed paper. Chill until firm.

Yield: 60 servings.   **Prep Time:** 10 minutes plus chilling.

EASY PEANUT BUTTER FUDGE

1 cup margarine
1 cup peanut butter
1 teaspoon vanilla extract
3 to 4 cups confectioners' sugar

Melt margarine in saucepan over low heat; remove from heat. Add peanut butter; mix well. Stir in vanilla. Add enough confectioners' sugar gradually to make stiff but not dry mixture, mixing well after each addition. Press into buttered 9x9-inch dish. Let stand until firm. Cut into squares.

Yield: 32 servings.   **Prep Time:** 10 minutes plus standing.

HAYSTACKS

12 ounces white chocolate
2 cups salted peanuts
1½ cups broken thin pretzel sticks

Melt chocolate in double boiler over simmering water, stirring constantly. Cool for 5 minutes. Add peanuts and pretzels; mix gently until coated. Drop by rounded teaspoonfuls onto foil. Let stand until cool. Store candies in refrigerator.

Yield: 36 servings.   **Prep Time:** 10 minutes plus standing.

KISS CANDIES

¾ cup finely chopped slivered almonds
½ cup confectioners' sugar
5 teaspoons light corn syrup
1 teaspoon almond extract
6 ounces milk chocolate kisses
1 cup sugar

Mix almonds and confectioners' sugar in bowl. Add mixture of corn syrup and almond extract gradually, mixing well. Tint with food coloring if desired. Shape by teaspoonfuls around chocolate kisses, maintaining kiss shape; roll in sugar. Store in airtight container.

Yield: 24 servings.   **Prep Time:** 15 minutes.

Substitute lower fat almonds for peanuts or
pecans in recipes calling for nuts.

CHOCOLATE-COVERED ORANGE SLICES

1   16-ounce package miniature candy orange slices
2 ounces paraffin
1 cup semisweet chocolate chips
2 ounces white chocolate candy coating

Place toothpick in each orange slice. Melt paraffin with chocolate chips in double boiler. Dip orange slices into melted chocolate. Place on wax paper-lined surface. Repeat process. Melt white chocolate in double boiler. Dip one end of each orange slice in white chocolate with toothpick. Place on waxed paper-lined surface. Let stand until firm. Place in paper bonbon cups.

Yield: 24 servings.   **Prep Time:** 20 minutes plus standing.

ORANGE AND CHOCOLATE TRUFFLES

2 oranges, ground
8 ounces semisweet chocolate
¼ cup margarine
¼ cup whipping cream
3 tablespoons sugar
1   12-ounce package vanilla wafers, crushed
1 cup shredded coconut
1 cup chopped pecans

Combine oranges, chocolate, margarine, whipping cream and sugar in heavy saucepan. Cook over low heat for 10 minutes, stirring constantly. Add vanilla wafer crumbs; mix well. Chill until firm. Shape into 1-inch balls. Coat with coconut or chopped pecans.

Yield: 48 servings.   **Prep Time:** 15 minutes plus chilling.

CHOCOLATE PEANUT CLUSTERS

6 ounces chocolate chips
2/3 cup sweetened condensed milk
1½ cups salted Spanish peanuts
1 teaspoon vanilla extract

Melt chocolate chips in double boiler over hot water, stirring until smooth. Remove from heat. Stir in condensed milk, peanuts and vanilla. Drop by teaspoonfuls onto waxed paper. Let stand for several hours or until firm. Store clusters in airtight container.

Yield: 24 servings.   **Prep Time:** 5 minutes plus standing.

PECAN TEMPTATIONS

18 ounces milk chocolate, broken into pieces
1   14-ounce can sweetened condensed milk
1   7-ounce jar marshmallow creme
42 marshmallows
1 pound pecans, finely chopped

Combine chocolate, condensed milk and marshmallow creme in double boiler. Cook over hot water until chocolate melts, stirring constantly; remove from heat. Keep warm. Dip each marshmallow into chocolate mixture with 2-prong fork, coating completely. Roll in pecans until completely covered. Place on foil-lined tray. Chill until firm. Place in paper bonbon cups. Store in airtight container. May also coat with coconut or candy sprinkles.

Yield: 42 servings.   **Prep Time:** 10 minutes plus chilling.

PRONTO PRALINES

1   4-ounce package vanilla pudding and pie filling mix
½ cup sugar
1 cup packed light brown sugar
1   5-ounce can evaporated milk
1 teaspoon vanilla extract
2 cups coarsely chopped pecans

Combine pudding mix, sugar and brown sugar in medium saucepan. Stir in evaporated milk. Bring to a boil, stirring constantly. Cook for 5 minutes, stirring occasionally; remove from heat. Stir in vanilla. Beat for 3 minutes or until still shiny; do not overbeat. Stir in pecans. Drop by tablespoonfuls onto waxed paper. Let stand for 1 hour or until firm. Store in airtight container.

Yield: 24 servings.   **Prep Time:** 10 minutes plus standing.

ROCKY ROAD CLUSTERS

16 ounces milk chocolate
3 cups miniature marshmallows
1 cup coarsely chopped pecans
½ cup semisweet miniature chocolate chips

Melt milk chocolate in double boiler over hot water. Remove from heat. Add marshmallows, pecans and chocolate chips; stir until coated. Drop by spoonfuls onto waxed paper. Let stand until firm. Store in cool place.

Yield: 32 servings.   **Prep Time:** 10 minutes plus standing.

Pudding mixes come in sugar-free versions with fewer carbohydrates.

TIGER BUTTER

1 cup white chocolate candy coating wafers
1/2 cup peanut butter
1 cup chocolate candy coating wafers

Melt white chocolate wafers in double boiler over hot water, stirring constantly. Blend in peanut butter. Melt chocolate wafers in second double boiler over hot water, stirring constantly. Alternate strips of peanut butter and chocolate mixtures on waxed paper-lined tray; swirl with knife. Let stand until firm. Break into pieces.

Yield: 20 servings.   **Prep Time:** 10 minutes standing.

MICROWAVE TOFFEE

1 cup sugar
1/2 cup light corn syrup
1/2 cup pecan halves
2 tablespoons margarine
1 teaspoon vanilla extract
1/2 teaspoon baking soda
1 cup semisweet chocolate chips
1/2 cup coarsely chopped pecans

Combine sugar and corn syrup in 2-quart glass bowl. Microwave on High in 700-watt microwave oven for 6 minutes, stirring once. Add pecan halves, margarine and vanilla; mix well. Microwave for 1 minute longer. Stir in baking soda. Spread on foil-lined surface. Sprinkle chocolate chips over hot candy. Let stand for 1 1/2 minutes. Spread chocolate over top. Sprinkle with coarsely chopped pecans. Chill until firm. Break into pieces. May substitute almonds, pistachios or walnuts for pecans.

Yield: 16 servings.   **Prep Time:** 10 minutes plus chilling.

TRIPLE-DECKER FUDGE

> 1 10-ounce package milk chocolate chunks
> 1 10-ounce package semisweet chocolate chunks
> 1 10-ounce package vanilla milk-flavored chips
> 2 14-ounce cans sweetened condensed milk

Place milk chocolate, semisweet chocolate and vanilla milk chips in separate microwave-safe bowls. Add ¾ cup condensed milk to each of the chocolate bowls. Pour remaining condensed milk into vanilla milk bowl. Microwave each bowl on High for 1 to 1¼ minutes or until melted; blend well. Layer milk chocolate, vanilla and semisweet chocolate in foil-lined 9x13-inch pan. Chill until firm. Remove from pan, peel off foil and cut into 1-inch squares. Place in paper bonbon cups. Store in refrigerator.

Yield: 96 servings.   **Prep Time:** 5 minutes plus chilling.

SPICED WALNUT BRITTLE

> 2 cups sugar
> ½ cup light corn syrup
> ¼ cup water
> 2 tablespoons margarine, softened
> 1½ teaspoons vanilla extract
> 1 teaspoon baking soda
> 1 teaspoon cinnamon
> 2 cups broken walnuts

Combine sugar, corn syrup and water in glass bowl. Microwave on High for 5 to 6 minutes or until mixture comes to a boil; stir. Microwave on High for 6 to 10 minutes or to 290 degrees on candy thermometer, hard-crack stage. Stir in margarine, vanilla, baking soda, cinnamon and walnuts. Spread on buttered tray. Let stand until firm. Break into pieces.

Yield: 24 servings.   **Prep Time:** 15 minutes plus standing.

CHOCOLATE-COVERED APPLES

8 large Granny Smith apples, stems removed
8 wooden popsicle sticks or skewers
1¹/₃ cups confectioners' sugar
¹/₂ cup unsweetened cocoa
¹/₂ cup vegetable oil
1 cup semisweet or milk chocolate chips
2 cups chopped white chocolate

Wash and dry apples. Insert popsicle stick into stem end of each apple. Place on waxed paper-lined tray. Combine confectioners' sugar, cocoa and oil in glass bowl; mix well. Add chocolate chips. Microwave on High for 1 minute; mix well. Microwave for 15 to 30 seconds longer if necessary to melt any remaining chips. Twirl apples in chocolate mixture or spoon mixture over apples; tap popsicle sticks on edge of pan to remove excess coating. Return to tray. Let stand for 5 minutes. Coat with white chocolate. Chill until firm. Store apples wrapped in plastic wrap. Cut apples in half to serve if desired. May substitute candy or nuts for white chocolate. May drizzle coated apples with melted caramel before coating as desired.

Yield: 16 servings.   **Prep Time:** 10 minutes plus standing.

CANDY HASH

4 cups Cap'n Crunch's Crunch Berries cereal
2 cups dry-roasted peanuts
2 cups slivered almonds
2 cups miniature marshmallows
1 pound white chocolate candy coating

Mix cereal, peanuts, almonds and marshmallows in large bowl. Melt candy coating in saucepan over low heat, stirring constantly. Pour over cereal mixture; mix well. Spread on baking sheet. Let stand until firm. Break into small pieces. Store in airtight container.

Yield: 20 servings.   **Prep Time:** 10 minutes plus standing.

CARAMEL CRACKERS

1/2 cup sugar
1/2 cup light corn syrup
1/4 cup margarine
1 teaspoon baking soda
1 teaspoon vanilla extract
1 16-ounce package oyster crackers
1 cup peanuts

Combine sugar, corn syrup and margarine in saucepan over low heat. Bring to a simmer. Cook for 5 minutes; remove from heat. Stir in baking soda and vanilla. Pour over crackers and peanuts in lightly greased 9x13-inch baking pan; toss to coat. Bake at 225 degrees until golden brown, stirring occasionally. Pour onto waxed paper to cool, stirring gently to separate. Store in airtight container.

Yield: 12 servings.   **Prep Time:** 10 minutes plus baking.

CHRISTMAS CRUNCH

1 cup peanut butter
1 cup chocolate syrup
1 12-ounce package Chex cereal
1 8-ounce package "M & M's" Plain red and
green Chocolate Candies
1 8-ounce package "M & M's" Peanut red and
green Chocolate Candies
2 cups confectioners' sugar
1 12-ounce jar mixed nuts

Combine peanut butter and chocolate syrup in glass bowl. Microwave on High for 2 minutes; stir until well mixed. Let stand until cool. Pour over cereal in large bowl; mix gently until coated. Pour cereal into paper bag. Add candies, confectioners' sugar and nuts. Fold top of sack over tightly. Shake until cereal is coated with confectioners' sugar. Store in airtight container.

Yield: 30 servings.   **Prep Time:** 15 minutes.

QUICK GRANOLA

1/2 cup sunflower oil   1/2 cup honey
1 cup packed light brown sugar
2 teaspoons cinnamon
2 teaspoons vanilla extract
6 cups old-fashioned oats   1 cup coconut
1/2 cup wheat germ   1/2 cup sunflower seed
1 cup chopped blanched almonds
1/2 cup dry milk powder   2/3 cup raisins
2/3 cup dried apples, chopped
2/3 cup dried apricots, chopped
2/3 cup dates, chopped
2/3 cup dried pineapple, chopped
1 cup "M & M's" Plain Chocolate Candies

Combine oil, honey, brown sugar, cinnamon and vanilla in large glass dish. Microwave on High for 4 to 5 minutes or until brown sugar melts, stirring once. Add oats, coconut, wheat germ, sunflower seed, almonds and milk powder; mix well. Divide into 2 portions. Place in glass casseroles. Microwave each portion for 6 minutes or until mixture begins to appear dry, stirring several times. Stir in raisins, apples, apricots, dates, pineapple and candies. Cool on waxed paper. Store in airtight container.

Yield: 24 servings.   **Prep Time:** 15 minutes.

EASY POPCORN BALLS

1 cup packed light brown sugar
8 cups miniature marshmallows
1/2 cup margarine   3 quarts popped popcorn

Combine brown sugar, marshmallows and margarine in saucepan; mix well. Cook over low heat until marshmallows are melted, stirring constantly. Pour over popcorn in large bowl; mix lightly. Shape into 20 balls. Place on waxed paper. Let stand until firm. Store in airtight container.

Yield: 20 servings.   **Prep Time:** 15 minutes plus standing.

POPCORN FANTASY

1 cup margarine
1   16-ounce package marshmallows
1 teaspoon vanilla extract
10 cups popped popcorn
1 cup mixed nuts
1   8-ounce package chopped dried fruit mix

Melt margarine and marshmallows in double boiler over hot water, stirring constantly. Remove from heat. Add vanilla. Combine popcorn, nuts and fruit in large bowl. Pour marshmallow mixture over top; mix well. Press into buttered 9x13-inch dish. Chill for several hours. Cut into squares.

Yield: 32 servings.   **Prep Time:** 10 minutes plus chilling.

PRALINE NIBBLES

½ cup margarine
¾ cup packed light brown sugar
1 cup pecans, broken
2 cups rice Chex
2 cups corn Chex
2 cups wheat Chex

Combine margarine and brown sugar in saucepan. Bring mixture to a boil over medium heat, stirring constantly. Cook for 2 minutes; remove from heat. Stir in pecans and cereal. Place in 9x13-inch baking pan. Bake at 325 degrees for 8 to 12 minutes, stirring several times. Cool on paper towels.

Yield: 15 servings.   **Prep Time:** 5 minutes plus baking.

*Cereals and popcorn are a great base for snacks
because of their low fat content.*

LIGHT ICED PRETZELS

2 egg whites
1/4 teaspoon cream of tartar
1/2 teaspoon vanilla extract
1 cup confectioners' sugar, sifted
8 ounces 3-ring pretzels
Colored sugar sprinkles

Beat egg whites with cream of tartar at high speed in mixer bowl until soft peaks form. Add vanilla. Add confectioners' sugar 1 tablespoon at a time, beating until stiff peaks form. Dip tops of pretzels into icing. Place iced side up on wire rack. Decorate with sugar sprinkles. Let stand until firm. Store in airtight container.

Yield: 40 servings. **Prep Time:** 15 minutes plus standing.

SUGAR AND SPICE SNACK

1 6-ounce package bugle-shaped corn snacks
2 cups mixed nuts
2 tablespoons orange juice
2 egg whites
1 1/3 cups sugar
1 tablespoon grated orange rind
1 teaspoon cinnamon
1 teaspoon allspice
1 teaspoon ginger

Mix corn snacks and nuts in large bowl. Beat orange juice and egg whites with wire whisk until foamy. Whisk in sugar, orange rind, cinnamon, allspice and ginger. Pour over nut mixture, tossing to coat. Spread in greased 10x15-inch baking pan. Bake at 275 degrees for 45 minutes, stirring every 15 minutes. Spread on waxed paper to cool, stirring gently to separate. Store in airtight container.

Yield: 20 servings. **Prep Time:** 10 minutes plus baking.

Sweet Crispmix

2 12-ounce packages Crispix cereal
2 cups pecan halves
2 cups whole blanched almonds
14 tablespoons margarine
2 cups packed light brown sugar
1 cup dark corn syrup
1½ to 2 teaspoons vanilla extract

Combine cereal, pecan halves and almonds in large roasting pan sprayed with nonstick cooking spray. Melt margarine in saucepan. Add brown sugar and corn syrup; mix well. Bring to a boil over low heat, stirring constantly; remove from heat. Stir in vanilla. Pour over cereal mixture; toss to coat. Bake at 250 degrees for 1 hour, stirring every 15 minutes. Spread on waxed paper. Let stand until cool. Break into pieces. Store in airtight container.

Yield: 40 servings.   **Prep Time:** 10 minutes plus baking.

White Chocolate Crunch

1 14-ounce package Honeycomb cereal
1 12-ounce package pretzels
12 ounces mixed nuts
1½ to 2 pounds white chocolate candy coating
Candy sprinkles

Mix cereal, pretzels and nuts in very large bowl. Melt white chocolate in double boiler over hot water. Pour over cereal; stir to coat well. Spread on waxed paper. Sprinkle with candy sprinkles. Cool completely. Store in airtight container.

Yield: 64 servings.   **Prep Time:** 10 minutes plus standing.

INCREDIBLE COOKIES

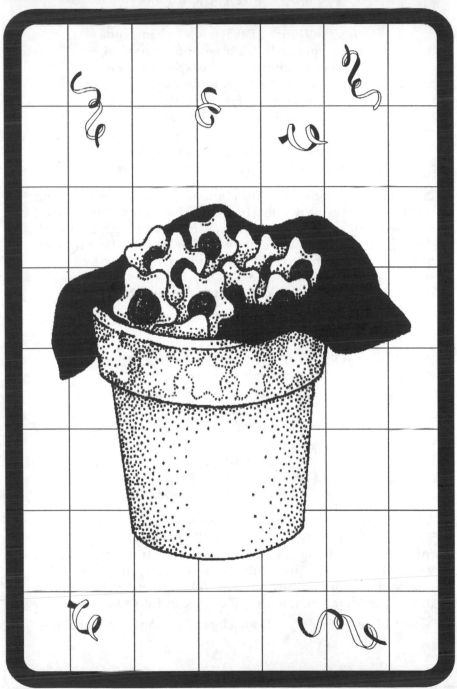

Nutritional information for Incredible Cookies is on pages 157–158.

APPLESAUCE RAISIN COOKIES

3¼ cups flour   1 teaspoon baking soda
1 teaspoon salt   1 teaspoon cinnamon
¼ teaspoon cloves   ¼ teaspoon nutmeg
¾ cup packed light brown sugar
1 cup margarine, softened   ¾ cup sugar
2 eggs, slightly beaten
½ cup applesauce
½ cup coarsely chopped pecans
1 cup raisins, plumped in hot water, drained

Sift flour, baking soda, salt, cinnamon, cloves and nutmeg together. Cream brown sugar, margarine and sugar in bowl with wooden spoon until light and fluffy. Add eggs; beat well. Add flour mixture alternately with applesauce, beating well after each addition. Stir in pecans and raisins. Drop by spoonfuls 2 inches apart on nonstick cookie sheet. Bake at 350 degrees for 12 minutes. Remove to wire rack to cool.

Yield: 42 servings.   **Prep Time:** 15 minutes plus baking.

APRICOT OATMEAL SQUARES

1 cup sugar   1½ cups flour
1½ cups oats
½ cup chopped pecans   ½ teaspoon salt
¾ cup margarine, softened
1 egg, lightly beaten
1 teaspoon vanilla extract
1   10-ounce jar apricot jam

Combine sugar, flour, oats, pecans, salt, margarine, egg and vanilla in bowl; mix with fork until crumbly. Reserve ¾ of mixture for topping. Press remaining mixture into greased 9x13-inch baking pan. Spread with jam; sprinkle with reserved crumb mixture. Bake at 350 degrees for 30 minutes or until golden. Let stand until cool. Cut into squares.

Yield: 24 servings.   **Prep Time:** 10 minutes plus baking.

BROWNIES

2 ounces chocolate
½ cup oil   2 eggs
1 cup sugar   1 cup flour
¼ teaspoon salt
1 teaspoon (scant) baking powder
1 teaspoon vanilla extract
1 cup chopped pecans

Melt chocolate in double boiler. Stir in oil. Cool for several minutes. Beat eggs in mixer bowl. Add sugar; mix well. Blend in chocolate mixture. Add flour, salt, baking powder and vanilla; mix well. Stir in pecans. Pour into greased 9x13-inch baking pan. Bake at 350 degrees for 20 minutes. Cool in pan for several minutes. Cut into bars.

Yield: 24 servings.   **Prep Time:** 10 minutes plus baking.

BLACK FOREST BROWNIES

¼ cup margarine
1 cup semisweet chocolate chips
2 cups baking mix
1   14-ounce can sweetened condensed milk
1 egg, beaten
1 teaspoon almond extract
1 cup semisweet chocolate chips
½ cup chopped candied cherries
½ cup sliced almonds, toasted

Melt margarine and 1 cup chocolate chips in large saucepan over low heat; remove from heat. Add baking mix, condensed milk, egg and almond extract; mix well. Stir in remaining 1 cup chocolate chips and cherries. Pour into greased 9x13-inch baking pan. Top with almonds. Bake at 350 degrees for 22 to 27 minutes or until brownies begin to pull away from side of pan. Brownies will be moist. Let stand until cool. Cut into bars. Store in tightly covered container at room temperature.

Yield: 18 servings.   **Prep Time:** 10 minutes plus baking.

CARAMEL SQUARES

1   20-ounce package brownie mix
½ cup semisweet chocolate chips
½ cup chopped pecans
20 caramels
3 tablespoons milk

Prepare brownie mix using package directions. Spread in greased 9x13-inch baking pan. Sprinkle with chocolate chips and pecans. Bake using package directions. Combine caramels and milk in small bowl. Microwave on High for 1 minute; mix well. Drizzle over brownies. Let stand until cool. Cut into squares.

Yield: 24 servings.   **Prep Time:** 10 minutes plus baking.

CHEESECAKE SQUARES

⅔ cup graham cracker crumbs
¼ cup sugar
½ cup chopped pecans
¼ cup flour
½ cup melted margarine
¼ cup sugar
8 ounces cream cheese, softened
1 egg, beaten

Combine graham cracker crumbs, ¼ cup sugar, pecans and flour in bowl; mix well. Stir in melted margarine. Press into 8x8-inch baking pan. Bake at 350 degrees for 12 minutes. Cream ¼ cup sugar and cream cheese in small mixer bowl. Add egg; beat until creamy. Pour over prepared crust. Bake at 350 degrees for 20 minutes or until firm. Cool on wire rack. Cut into squares.

Yield: 36 servings.   **Prep Time:** 10 minutes plus baking.

CHERRY WINKS

2¼ cups sifted flour   1 teaspoon baking powder
½ teaspoon baking soda   ½ teaspoon salt
1 cup chopped pecans   1 cup finely chopped dates
⅓ cup finely chopped maraschino cherries
¾ cup butter, softened   1 cup sugar
2 eggs   2 tablespoons milk
1 teaspoon vanilla extract
⅔ cup cornflake crumbs
15 maraschino cherries, cut into quarters

Sift flour, baking powder, baking soda and salt together. Add pecans, dates and ⅓ cup cherries; toss to coat well. Cream butter and sugar in mixer bowl until light and fluffy. Add eggs 1 at a time, beating well after each addition. Add milk and vanilla; mix well. Stir in floured fruit. Shape by spoonfuls into balls. Roll in cornflake crumbs. Place on greased cookie sheet; top with 1 maraschino cherry quarter. Bake at 350 degrees for 12 minutes or until light brown. Remove to wire rack to cool.

Yield: 60 servings.   **Prep Time:** 15 minutes plus baking.

CHOCOLATE CHIP COOKIES

1¼ cups margarine, softened   2 cups sugar
2 eggs   1 teaspoon vanilla extract
2 cups flour   ¾ cup baking cocoa
1 teaspoon baking soda
½ teaspoon salt   1 cup chocolate chips

Cream margarine and sugar in mixer bowl until light and fluffy. Add eggs and vanilla; mix well. Add mixture of flour, cocoa, baking soda and salt; mix well. Stir in chocolate chips. Drop by teaspoonfuls 2 inches apart on nonstick cookie sheet. Bake at 350 degrees for 9 minutes. Cool on cookie sheet for 2 minutes. Remove to wire rack to cool completely.

Yield: 36 servings.   **Prep Time:** 10 minutes plus baking.

CRANBERRY TASSIES

3 ounces cream cheese, softened
½ cup margarine, softened   1 cup sifted flour
1 egg, beaten
¾ cup packed light brown sugar
1 tablespoon butter
1 teaspoon vanilla extract   ⅛ teaspoon salt
⅔ cup coarsely broken pecans
1 cup cranberries, chopped

Blend cream cheese and ½ cup margarine in bowl. Add flour; mix well. Chill in refrigerator. Shape cream cheese mixture into 1-inch balls. Press over bottoms and sides of greased miniature muffin cups. Beat egg, brown sugar and 1 tablespoon butter in mixer bowl until light and fluffy. Beat in vanilla and salt. Sprinkle pecans and cranberries into prepared muffin cups. Fill with egg mixture. Bake at 325 degrees for 25 minutes or until filling is set. Cool.

Yield: 24 servings.   **Prep Time:** 20 minutes plus baking.

CHRISTMAS DOLLIES

1½ cups graham cracker crumbs
2 tablespoons sugar
½ cup melted margarine
2 cups miniature marshmallows
1 cup maraschino cherries
1½ cups coconut
1   14-ounce can sweetened condensed milk
1 cup chopped pecans

Mix graham cracker crumbs, sugar and margarine in bowl. Press into 9x13-inch baking dish. Layer marshmallows, cherries and coconut in prepared dish. Drizzle evenly with condensed milk. Press pecans into top. Bake at 350 degrees for 25 minutes.

Yield: 24 servings.   **Prep Time:** 10 minutes plus baking.

FRUITCAKE BALLS

3 cups chopped dates
8 ounces candied red cherries, chopped
8 ounces candied green cherries, chopped
2   3-ounce cans coconut
1   14-ounce can sweetened condensed milk
4 cups chopped pecans

Mix dates, cherries, coconut, condensed milk and pecans in bowl. Shape into 1-inch balls. Place on lightly greased cookie sheet. Bake at 300 degrees for 25 minutes. Cool on cookie sheet for 2 minutes. Remove to wire rack to cool completely.

Yield: 72 servings.   **Prep Time:** 5 minutes plus baking.

GINGERSNAPS

3/4 cup shortening
1 cup sugar
1/4 cup molasses
1 egg
2 cups flour
2 teaspoons baking soda
1 teaspoon cinnamon
1 teaspoon ground cloves
1 teaspoon ginger
1/2 cup sugar

Cream shortening and 1 cup sugar in mixer bowl until light and fluffy. Add molasses and egg; beat well. Sift flour and baking soda into mixture; stir well. Add cinnamon, cloves and ginger; mix well. Shape dough into 1-inch balls. Roll in 1/2 cup sugar to coat. Arrange on nonstick cookie sheet. Bake at 350 degrees for 10 to 12 minutes or until golden brown. Cool on wire rack.

Yield: 72 servings.   **Prep Time:** 15 minutes plus baking.

ICE CREAM COOKIES

2 cups margarine, softened
4 cups flour
1 pint vanilla ice cream, softened
2 cups confectioners' sugar
1   10-ounce jar strawberry preserves

Cut margarine into flour in bowl until crumbly. Mix in ice cream. Chill overnight. Roll dough on surface sprinkled with ¼-inch confectioners' sugar. Cut as desired. Make indentation in center of each cookie. Fill with preserves. Place on cookie sheet. Bake at 350 degrees for 15 minutes or until edges start to brown. Remove to wire rack to cool. Spoon additional confectioners' sugar into tea strainer. Sprinkle over cookies.

Yield: 72 servings.   **Prep Time:** 20 minutes plus baking.

LACE COOKIES

½ cup ground blanched almonds
½ cup butter
½ cup sugar
1 tablespoon flour
2 tablespoons milk

Combine almonds, butter, sugar, flour and milk in saucepan. Cook over low heat until butter is melted, stirring constantly. Drop by teaspoonfuls onto greased and floured cookie sheets, allowing only 4 to 6 cookies to each cookie sheet. Bake at 375 degrees for 6 minutes or until cookies are light brown and centers are bubbly. Let stand on cookie sheet for 1 minute. Remove gently to wire rack to cool completely.

Yield: 60 servings.   **Prep Time:** 10 minutes plus baking.

LADYFINGERS

1/2 cup margarine, softened
1 tablespoon sugar
1 1/2 teaspoons vanilla extract
1 cup flour
1/2 cup finely chopped pecans
1/3 cup confectioners' sugar

Cream margarine and sugar in mixer bowl until light and fluffy. Add vanilla; mix well. Combine flour and pecans in bowl. Add to creamed mixture; stir well. Shape into thumb-sized bars. Place on nonstick cookie sheet. Bake at 350 degrees for 15 minutes. Roll warm cookies in confectioners' sugar to coat. Cool on wire rack.

Yield: 24 servings.   **Prep Time:** 15 minutes plus baking.

LEMON BARS

1   2-layer package yellow cake mix
1/2 cup margarine, softened
1 egg, beaten
1 teaspoon lemon juice
1   1-pound package confectioners' sugar
8 ounces cream cheese, softened
1 teaspoon lemon juice
2 eggs, beaten

Combine cake mix, margarine, egg and 1 teaspoon lemon juice in large bowl; mix well. Spread mixture in greased 9x13-inch baking pan. Cream confectioners' sugar with cream cheese in mixer bowl until light and fluffy. Add 1 teaspoon lemon juice; mix well. Add eggs, beating until mixture is creamy. Spread over cake mix mixture. Bake at 300 degrees for 20 to 25 minutes or until firm. Cool in pan; cut into bars.

Yield: 36 servings.   **Prep Time:** 15 minutes plus baking.

MINCEMEAT SQUARES

3/4 cup margarine, softened
3 tablespoons confectioners' sugar
1 1/2 cups flour
1/2 cup packed light brown sugar
1/3 cup margarine, softened   2 eggs, beaten
1 1/2 cups mincemeat   3/4 cup flaked coconut
1/3 cup chopped walnuts

Combine 3/4 cup margarine, confectioners' sugar and flour in bowl; mix well. Spread in greased 9x13-inch baking pan. Bake at 350 degrees for 10 minutes. Cool completely. Cream brown sugar and 1/3 cup margarine in mixer bowl until light and fluffy. Beat in eggs. Stir in mincemeat, coconut and walnuts. Spread over baked layer. Bake for 20 to 25 minutes or until set. Cool on wire rack. Cut into squares.

Yield: 30 servings.   **Prep Time:** 15 minutes plus baking.

MOLASSES DROP COOKIES

1/2 cup shortening   1/2 cup sugar
1/2 cup molasses   1 egg, beaten
1 teaspoon baking soda
1/2 cup buttermilk
2 1/2 cups flour, sifted
1 1/2 teaspoons cinnamon
1/2 teaspoon ginger   1/2 teaspoon salt
1/4 teaspoon cloves   1/2 cup raisins

Cream shortening and sugar in mixer bowl until light and fluffy. Add molasses and egg; mix well. Dissolve baking soda in buttermilk. Add flour, cinnamon, ginger, salt and cloves to creamed mixture alternately with buttermilk, mixing well after each addition. Add raisins; mix well. Drop by teaspoonfuls onto greased cookie sheet. Bake at 350 degrees for 12 minutes. Remove to wire rack to cool.

Yield: 42 servings.   **Prep Time:** 15 minutes plus baking.

GRANDMA'S OATMEAL COOKIES

1 cup raisins   1 cup sugar
1 cup shortening   2 eggs, beaten
1 teaspoon vanilla extract
2 cups flour   1 teaspoon baking soda
1/2 teaspoon salt   1 teaspoon cinnamon
1/4 teaspoon nutmeg
2 cups quick-cooking oats

Combine raisins and water to cover in saucepan. Bring to a boil; drain, reserving 6 tablespoons liquid. Cream sugar and shortening in mixer bowl until light and fluffy. Add eggs, vanilla and reserved raisin liquid; mix well. Sift in flour, baking soda, salt and spices; mix well. Stir in oats and raisins. Drop by teaspoonfuls onto greased cookie sheet. Bake at 350 degrees for 15 minutes or until brown.

Yield: 48 servings.   **Prep Time:** 15 minutes plus baking.

ONE-CUP COOKIES

1 cup margarine, softened
1 cup sugar   1 cup packed brown sugar
3 eggs   1 cup peanut butter
1 cup flour   1 tablespoon baking soda
1 cup oats   1 cup coconut
1 cup chopped walnuts
1 cup raisins
1 cup chocolate chips

Cream margarine, sugar and brown sugar in large mixer bowl until light and fluffy. Beat in eggs 1 at a time. Beat in peanut butter. Add mixture of flour and baking soda; mix well. Add oats, coconut, walnuts, raisins and chocolate chips in order listed, mixing well after each addition. Drop by heaping teaspoonfuls onto cookie sheet. Bake at 350 degrees for 10 minutes.

Yield: 60 servings.   **Prep Time:** 10 minutes plus baking.

MAGIC COOKIES

1 cup sugar
1 cup peanut butter
1 egg
48 chocolate star candies

Combine sugar, peanut butter and egg in bowl; mix well. Shape into 1-inch balls. Place on cookie sheet; press chocolate star into center of each cookie. Bake at 350 degrees for 6 minutes. Cool on wire rack.

Yield: 48 servings.   **Prep Time:** 5 minutes plus baking.

PEANUT BUTTER COOKIES

1¼ cups sifted flour
½ teaspoon salt
1 teaspoon cinnamon
½ teaspoon baking soda
½ cup margarine, softened
½ cup packed brown sugar
½ cup sugar
½ cup peanut butter
1 egg
1 teaspoon vanilla extract

Sift flour, salt, cinnamon and baking soda together. Cream margarine, brown sugar, sugar, peanut butter, egg and vanilla in mixer bowl until light and fluffy. Add sifted dry ingredients. Beat at low speed until moistened. Beat for 1 minute longer. Shape by 2 teaspoonfuls into balls. Place on greased cookie sheet. Flatten with fork dipped in flour. Bake at 350 degrees for 10 minutes or until brown. Remove to wire rack to cool.

Yield: 72 servings.   **Prep Time:** 10 minutes plus baking.

PECAN DREAMS

2 cups packed brown sugar
2 egg whites, stiffly beaten
2 tablespoons flour
Salt to taste
2 cups chopped pecans

Beat brown sugar into stiffly beaten egg whites in mixer bowl. Fold in flour, salt and pecans. Drop by spoonfuls onto greased cookie sheet. Bake at 325 degrees for 8 to 10 minutes or just until light brown. Remove to wire rack to cool.

Yield: 24 servings.   **Prep Time:** 10 minutes plus baking.

PINEAPPLE HAWAIIAN KISSES

1 cup confectioners' sugar
1 cup margarine
2 teaspoons vanilla extract
1/2 teaspoon salt
2 cups flour
1 1/2 cups finely chopped macadamia nuts
8 ounces cream cheese with pineapple, softened
2/3 cup flaked coconut, toasted

Cream confectioners' sugar and margarine in mixer bowl until light and fluffy. Add vanilla and salt; mix well. Add flour. Beat at low speed until blended. Shape by teaspoonfuls into balls; roll in macadamia nuts. Place on greased baking sheet. Make indentation in each cookie with thumb. Bake at 350 degrees for 12 to 14 minutes or until lightly browned and crisp. Remove to wire rack to cool. Fill indentations with cream cheese; sprinkle with coconut. Store in airtight container.

Yield: 72 servings.   **Prep Time:** 10 minutes plus baking.

PISTACHIO ICEBOX COOKIES

½ cup margarine, softened
1 cup sugar
1 teaspoon vanilla extract
1 egg
1½ cups flour
½ teaspoon baking powder
½ cup chopped pistachios

Cream margarine and sugar in mixer bowl until light and fluffy. Add vanilla and egg; mix well. Add mixture of flour and baking powder; mix well. Mix in pistachios. Shape into two 1¼-inch diameter rolls. Wrap in waxed paper or plastic wrap. Chill in refrigerator for up to 1 week. Slice cookie dough into ¼-inch slices; arrange on greased cookie sheet. Bake at 400 degrees for 6 to 7 minutes or until very light brown on edges. Cool on cookie sheet for 1 minute. Remove to wire rack to cool completely.

Yield: 72 servings.   **Prep Time:** 15 minutes plus baking.

POTATO CHIP SHORTBREAD COOKIES

2 cups margarine, softened
1 cup sugar
2 teaspoons vanilla extract
3 cups flour
1 cup chopped pecans
2 cups crushed potato chips
2 cups (or more) confectioners' sugar

Cream margarine, sugar and vanilla in mixer bowl until light and fluffy. Add flour; mix well. Stir in pecans and potato chips. Drop by teaspoonfuls onto nonstick cookie sheet. Bake at 350 degrees for 10 to 15 minutes or until golden. Sprinkle with confectioners' sugar. Cool on wire rack.

Yield: 84 servings.   **Prep Time:** 10 minutes plus baking.

PUMPKIN BARS

4 eggs   1²/₃ cups sugar
1 cup oil   2 cups cooked pumpkin
2 cups flour   1 teaspoon baking soda
2 teaspoons pumpkin pie spice
1 teaspoon baking powder
¹/₂ cup butter, softened
8 ounces cream cheese, softened
1 teaspoon vanilla extract
1   1-pound package confectioners' sugar

Beat eggs, sugar and oil in mixer bowl. Add pumpkin; beat until light and fluffy. Add mixture of flour, baking soda, pumpkin pie spice and baking powder; mix well. Spread in ungreased 10x15-inch baking pan. Bake at 350 degrees for 25 minutes. Cool in pan. Cream butter, cream cheese and vanilla in mixer bowl until light and fluffy. Add confectioners' sugar, beating until smooth. Spread over baked layer. Cut into bars.

Yield: 24 servings.   **Prep Time:** 10 minutes plus baking.

RASPBERRY THUMBPRINTS

1 cup unsalted butter, softened
¹/₂ cup sugar   2 cups flour
2 egg yolks
2 egg whites, lightly beaten
1 cup chopped walnuts
1   11-ounce jar seedless raspberry jam

Cream butter and sugar in mixer bowl until light and fluffy. Add flour and egg yolks. Beat for 1 minute. Shape into 1-inch balls. Dip into egg whites; roll in walnuts. Place 1¹/₂ inches apart on greased cookie sheet. Flatten to ¹/₄-inch thickness with glass. Make indentation in each cookie with thumb. Fill indentations with jam. Bake at 325 degrees for 12 to 15 minutes or until light brown. Store in covered container.

Yield: 36 servings.   **Prep Time:** 15 minutes plus baking.

SCOTTISH SHORTBREAD

1 cup butter, softened
1 cup margarine, softened
1 cup sugar
3/4 cup cornstarch
4½ cups flour
½ teaspoon baking powder

Mix butter, margarine and sugar in bowl with fork. Add cornstarch, flour and baking powder. Mix with wooden spoon until mixture forms ball. Press into 9x13-inch baking pan; prick with fork. Bake at 250 degrees for 2 hours. Cut into bars while warm.

Yield: 20 servings. **Prep Time:** 15 minutes plus baking.

SESAME COOKIES

2 cups margarine, softened
1¼ cups sugar
3 cups flour
1 cup sesame seed
2 cups shredded coconut
½ cup finely chopped almonds

Cream margarine and sugar in mixer bowl until light and fluffy. Add flour; mix well. Fold in sesame seed, coconut and almonds. Divide dough into 3 portions. Chill, covered, until firm. Shape dough into balls. Place on cookie sheet. Flatten with bottom of glass dipped in sugar. Bake at 300 degrees for 30 minutes. Remove to wire rack to cool completely.

Yield: 48 servings. **Prep Time:** 15 minutes plus baking.

SNICKERDOODLES

1 cup butter, softened
1½ cups sugar
2 eggs
1 teaspoon vanilla extract
2¾ cups flour
2 teaspoons cream of tartar
1 teaspoon baking soda
½ teaspoon salt
¼ cup sugar
2 tablespoons cinnamon

Cream butter, 1½ cups sugar, eggs and vanilla in mixer bowl until light and fluffy. Sift flour, cream of tartar, baking soda and salt together. Add to creamed mixture; mix well. Shape into small balls. Roll in mixture of ¼ cup sugar and cinnamon. Place on greased cookie sheet. Bake at 375 degrees for 8 to 10 minutes or until set. Cool on wire rack.

Yield: 96 servings.   **Prep Time:** 10 minutes plus baking.

SNICKERS COOKIES

1 large package refrigerator chocolate
chip cookie dough
5 or 6 Snickers candy bars, sliced ¼ inch thick

Spread cookie dough in 9x11-inch baking pan. Bake using package directions or until just golden brown. Arrange candy over baked layer. Bake until candy is softened; spread evenly over baked layer. Cool. Cut into squares.

Yield: 24 servings.   **Prep Time:** 5 minutes plus baking.

SOUR CREAM COOKIES

2 cups sugar
1 cup margarine, softened
1 cup sour cream
2 eggs, beaten
1 teaspoon vanilla extract
1 teaspoon baking soda
2 to 4 cups flour

Cream sugar and margarine in mixer bowl until light and creamy. Add sour cream and eggs; mix well. Add vanilla; mix well. Add mixture of baking soda and 1 cup flour; mix well. Add enough remaining flour to make dough. Knead 1/3 at a time on floured surface, kneading in any remaining flour needed for desired consistency. Roll and cut with cookie cutters. Place on cookie sheet. Bake at 375 degrees for 10 to 12 minutes or until brown. Remove to wire rack to cool.

Yield: 108 servings.   **Prep Time:** 15 minutes plus baking.

SUGAR COOKIES

1 cup butter, softened
1 cup corn oil
1 cup sugar
1 cup confectioners' sugar
2 eggs
4 cups flour
1 teaspoon baking soda
1 teaspoon cream of tartar
1 teaspoon vanilla extract

Cream butter, oil, sugar and confectioners' sugar in mixer bowl until light and fluffy. Add eggs; mix well. Sift in flour, baking soda and cream of tartar. Add vanilla; mix well. Drop by teaspoonfuls onto ungreased cookie sheet. Bake at 350 degrees for 10 minutes or until golden brown. May sprinkle with red and green sugar before baking for holiday cookies.

Yield: 48 servings.   **Prep Time:** 10 minutes plus baking.

OLD-FASHIONED TEA CAKES

1 cup butter, softened
2 cups sugar
3 eggs
2 tablespoons buttermilk
5 cups flour
1 teaspoon baking soda
1 teaspoon vanilla extract
½ cup sugar

Cream butter in mixer bowl until fluffy. Add 2 cups sugar. Beat until light. Add eggs 1 at a time, beating well after each addition. Add buttermilk; mix well. Stir in mixture of flour and baking soda gradually. Add vanilla; mix well. Chill for several hours to overnight. Roll ¼ inch thick on lightly floured surface. Cut with 3½-inch round cookie cutter. Place on lightly greased cookie sheet. Sprinkle with remaining ½ cup sugar. Bake at 400 degrees for 7 to 8 minutes or until edges are lightly browned. Remove to wire rack to cool.

Yield: 48 servings.   **Prep Time:** 15 minutes plus baking.

TOFFEE BARS

1 cup margarine, softened
1 cup packed light brown sugar
1 egg yolk
1 teaspoon vanilla extract
2 cups flour
6   1½-ounce bars chocolate
½ to 1 cup chopped pecans

Combine margarine, brown sugar, egg yolk, vanilla and flour in bowl; mix well. Spread in 10x15-inch baking pan. Bake at 350 degrees for 20 minutes. Place chocolate bars on hot baked layer; let stand until softened. Spread chocolate evenly; sprinkle with pecans. Cool; cut into bars.

Yield: 60 servings.   **Prep Time:** 5 minutes plus baking.

WHITE CHOCOLATE CHUNK COOKIES

1¼ cups unsalted margarine, softened
1 cup sugar   1 cup packed dark brown sugar
2 eggs   2 tablespoons milk
2 tablespoons vanilla extract
2½ cups flour   1 teaspoon baking powder
1 teaspoon baking soda   1 teaspoon salt
1 cup oats, pulverized   2 cups vanilla milk chips
1½ cups coarsely chopped pistachios

Cream margarine, sugar and brown sugar in mixer bowl until light and fluffy. Beat in eggs, milk and vanilla. Add mixture of flour, baking powder, baking soda, salt and oats gradually, mixing well after each addition. Stir in vanilla chips and 1 cup pistachios. Drop by heaping teaspoonfuls 2 inches apart onto greased cookie sheet. Sprinkle with remaining ½ cup pistachios; press lightly. Bake at 350 degrees for 8 to 10 minutes or until golden brown. Cool on cookie sheet for several minutes. Remove to wire rack to cool completely.

Yield: 84 servings.   **Prep Time:** 10 minutes plus baking.

YUM-YUM BARS

1   2-layer package German chocolate cake mix
⅓ cup evaporated milk   ¾ cup melted margarine
1 cup chocolate chips   1 cup chopped nuts
1   14-ounce package caramels   ⅓ cup evaporated milk

Combine cake mix, ⅓ cup evaporated milk and margarine in bowl; mix well. Spread half the mixture in 9x13-inch baking pan. Bake at 350 degrees for 6 minutes. Sprinkle with chocolate chips and nuts. Melt caramels in remaining ⅓ cup evaporated milk in saucepan, stirring constantly. Pour over chocolate chips and nuts. Top with remaining cake mix mixture. Bake for 15 to 20 minutes longer; do not overbake. Cool. Cut into bars.

Yield: 24 servings.   **Prep Time:** 10 minutes plus baking.

SCRUMPTIOUS DESSERTS

Nutritional information for Scrumptious Desserts is on pages 158–160.

ALMOST GUILT-FREE DESSERT

1 cup seedless grapes
1 cup strawberries
1 cup chopped bananas
1 cup chopped pineapple
1 cup chopped apple
½ cup fresh blueberries
2 cups vanilla yogurt
½ cup honey
1 teaspoon cinnamon
½ cup chopped walnuts or pecans
Coconut to taste

Combine grapes, strawberries, bananas, pineapple, apple and blueberries in large bowl; toss lightly. Combine yogurt, honey, cinnamon, walnuts or pecans and coconut in small bowl; mix well. Place fruit in individual serving bowls. Top with yogurt mixture or dip fruit into yogurt mixture.

Yield: 10 servings.   **Prep Time:** 10 minutes.

AMBROSIA GRATIN

1 16-ounce can Bartlett pear halves, drained
2 medium oranges, peeled, sliced crosswise
1 tablespoon honey
1 teaspoon lemon juice
2 teaspoons sliced almonds, toasted
2 teaspoons coconut, toasted

Slice pears into fans. Arrange orange slices in 2 small gratin dishes. Place pear fans over oranges. Drizzle with mixture of honey and lemon juice. Broil 3 to 5 inches from heat source for 6 to 8 minutes or until fruit is lightly browned. Sprinkle with almonds and coconut.

Yield: 2 servings.   **Prep Time:** 15 minutes.

APPLE CRISP

½ cup margarine   1 cup self-rising flour
1 cup quick-cooking oats
¾ cup packed brown sugar
6 cups sliced peeled apples
½ cup packed brown sugar   1 teaspoon cinnamon

Microwave margarine in 8x8-inch glass dish on High for 1 minute or until melted. Add flour, oats and ¾ cup brown sugar; mix well. Reserve half the mixture. Press remaining mixture firmly into dish. Spoon apples in prepared dish. Sprinkle with ½ cup brown sugar and cinnamon. Top with reserved oats mixture. Microwave, covered with plastic wrap, on High for 9 to 12 minutes.

Yield: 9 servings.   **Prep Time:** 15 minutes.

CREAMY COCONUT-APPLE CRUNCH

½ cup milk
1   4-ounce package coconut cream pudding
and pie filling mix
3 cups sliced cooking apples
½ cup melted margarine
1 cup flour   1 cup sugar
1 teaspoon baking powder
1 teaspoon cinnamon
½ teaspoon salt
½ teaspoon vanilla extract
1 egg   ½ cup chopped pecans

Combine milk and ½ of the pie filling mix in large mixer bowl; beat well. Add apples; mix well. Pour into 8-inch square baking pan. Combine margarine, flour, sugar, remaining pie filling mix, baking powder, cinnamon, salt, vanilla and egg in bowl; mix well. Fold in pecans. Spread over apple mixture. Bake at 350 degrees for 35 to 40 minutes or until apples are tender and topping is light golden brown.

Yield: 12 servings.   **Prep Time:** 15 minutes plus baking.

APPLE DUMPLINGS

2 Granny Smith apples
1　8-count can crescent rolls
1/8 teaspoon cinnamon
1/2 cup margarine
1 cup sugar
1 cup orange juice
1 teaspoon grated lemon rind
1 teaspoon vanilla extract

Peel and core apples; cut into fourths. Unroll and separate crescent rolls. Wrap each piece of apple in 1 crescent roll. Place in 8-inch square baking dish. Sprinkle with cinnamon. Combine margarine, sugar and orange juice in saucepan. Bring to a boil. Stir in lemon rind and vanilla. Pour over rolls. Bake at 350 degrees for 30 minutes. Spoon pan juices over rolls when serving.

Yield: 6 servings.　　　**Prep Time:** 15 minutes plus baking.

CREAMY APPLE SQUARES

1　2-layer package pudding-recipe yellow cake mix
1/2 cup margarine, softened
1/4 cup packed brown sugar
1/2 teaspoon cinnamon
2/3 cup thinly sliced apples
1 cup sour cream
1 egg

Combine cake mix and margarine in bowl; mix until crumbly. Press 1/3 cup mixture into 9x13-inch baking dish. Stir brown sugar and cinnamon into remaining mixture. Arrange apples in prepared dish. Spread with mixture of sour cream and egg. Sprinkle with remaining crumbs. Bake at 350 degrees for 25 to 30 minutes.

Yield: 15 servings.　　　**Prep Time:** 15 minutes plus baking.

BANANA SPLIT DESSERT

½ cup melted margarine
2 cups crushed graham crackers
2 cups confectioners' sugar
1 cup melted margarine
1 16-ounce can crushed pineapple, drained
3 or 4 bananas, sliced
8 ounces whipped topping
½ cup chopped pecans
¼ cup maraschino cherries

Mix ½ cup melted margarine and graham cracker crumbs in bowl. Press into 9x13-inch glass dish. Combine confectioners' sugar and 1 cup melted margarine in bowl; mix well. Spread over crumb crust. Layer pineapple, banana slices, whipped topping, pecans and maraschino cherries in dish. Chill in refrigerator overnight.

Yield: 15 servings.   **Prep Time:** 15 minutes plus chilling.

BLACKBERRY FLUFF

1 21-ounce can blackberry pie filling
8 ounces whipped topping
1 14-ounce can sweetened condensed milk
1 8-ounce can crushed pineapple
1 cup chopped pecans

Combine pie filling, whipped topping, condensed milk, pineapple and pecans in large bowl; mix well. Chill for several hours to overnight. May substitute other flavors of pie filling for blackberry.

Yield: 10 servings.   **Prep Time:** 5 minutes plus chilling.

BLUEBERRY-GRAPE COMPOTE

1/4 cup sugar
1/4 cup water
1/2 teaspoon grated lime rind
1/4 cup lime juice
2 cups blueberries
2 cups seedless grape halves
2 kiwifruit, peeled, sliced

Combine sugar, water and lime rind in saucepan; mix well. Cook over medium heat until sugar dissolves, stirring frequently. Stir in lime juice. Cool to room temperature. Combine with blueberries and grapes in bowl; mix well. Chill, covered, until serving time, stirring occasionally. Top with kiwifruit at serving time.

Yield: 6 servings.   **Prep Time:** 10 minutes plus chilling.

MIDSUMMER BERRIES

1 10-ounce package butter cookies
3/4 cup margarine, softened
1 cup confectioners' sugar
2 eggs
1/3 cup chopped walnuts
1 quart blueberries
1 cup unsweetened whipped cream

Process cookies into crumbs in blender container. Sprinkle half the crumbs in 9-inch square dish. Cream margarine and confectioners' sugar in mixer bowl until light and fluffy. Add eggs 1 at a time, beating well after each addition. Spread in prepared dish. Sprinkle with walnuts; top with blueberries. Spread whipped cream over blueberries. Sprinkle with remaining crumbs. Chill for 2 hours. Cut into squares.

Yield: 12 servings.   **Prep Time:** 15 minutes plus chilling.

BUTTERFINGER DESSERT

2 eggs   2 cups confectioners' sugar
½ cup melted margarine
9 ounces whipped topping
2 large Butterfinger candy bars, crushed
1 medium angel food cake, torn into bite-sized pieces

Beat eggs in mixer bowl. Add confectioners' sugar and margarine; beat well. Fold in whipped topping. Reserve ¼ of the candy bar crumbs. Add remaining crumbs to whipped topping mixture. Alternate layers of cake pieces and whipped topping mixture in 9x13-inch glass dish. Sprinkle with reserved crumbs. Freeze until firm.

Yield: 12 servings.   **Prep Time:** 15 minutes plus freezing.

LATTICE CHERRY CHEESECAKE

1   17-ounce package refrigerator sugar cookie dough
16 ounces cream cheese, softened
1 cup sour cream
¾ cup sugar
¼ teaspoon almond extract
3 eggs
1   21-ounce can cherry pie filling

Cut cookie dough into ⅛-inch slices. Place slices, overlapping slightly, over bottom and side of greased 9-inch springform pan. Seal edges to form shell. Combine cream cheese, sour cream, sugar and almond extract in mixer bowl; mix well. Add eggs 1 at a time, mixing well after each addition. Reserve ¼ cup mixture. Spoon remaining mixture into prepared pan. Bake at 350 degrees for 70 minutes. Remove from oven. Spoon pie filling over cheesecake layer. Spread reserved cream cheese mixture in lattice-design on top. Increase temperature to 450 degrees. Bake for 10 minutes. Loosen cheesecake from pan with knife. Cool for 30 minutes. Remove side of pan.

Yield: 12 servings.   **Prep Time:** 15 minutes plus baking.

PETITE CHERRY CHEESECAKES

24 vanilla wafers
16 ounces cream cheese, softened
2 eggs
1/4 cup lemon juice
1 tablespoon vanilla extract
3/4 cup sugar
1   21-ounce can cherry pie filling

Place 1 vanilla wafer in each paper-lined muffin cup. Combine cream cheese, eggs, lemon juice, vanilla and sugar in bowl; mix well. Spoon onto vanilla wafers. Bake at 350 degrees for 15 to 20 minutes or until set. Let stand until cool. Top with pie filling.

Yield: 24 servings.   **Prep Time:** 10 minutes plus baking.

CHOCOLATE CHIP CHEESECAKE

1 1/2 cups finely crushed chocolate creme-filled cookies
2 to 3 tablespoons melted margarine
24 ounces cream cheese, softened
1   14-ounce can sweetened condensed milk
3 eggs
2 teaspoons vanilla extract
1 cup miniature chocolate chips
1 teaspoon flour

Mix crumbs with margarine in bowl. Press over bottom of 9-inch springform pan. Beat cream cheese in bowl until light and fluffy. Add condensed milk gradually, beating until smooth. Add eggs and vanilla; beat well. Toss 1/2 cup chocolate chips with flour to coat; fold into cream cheese mixture. Pour into prepared pan. Sprinkle remaining 1/2 cup chocolate chips over top. Bake at 300 degrees for 55 to 60 minutes or until set. Cool. Chill in refrigerator.

Yield: 16 servings.   **Prep Time:** 15 minutes plus baking.

MINT CHOCOLATE CHIP CHEESECAKE

1½ cups fine Hydrox cookie crumbs
2 tablespoons melted margarine
24 ounces cream cheese, softened
1   14-ounce can sweetened condensed milk   3 eggs
2 teaspoons vanilla extract   ½ cup mint chocolate chips
1 teaspoon flour   ½ cup mint chocolate chips

Mix crumbs and melted margarine in bowl. Press over bottom of 9-inch springform pan. Beat cream cheese in mixer bowl until light and fluffy. Add condensed milk gradually, beating until smooth. Beat in eggs and vanilla. Toss ½ cup chocolate chips with flour. Stir into batter. Spoon into prepared pan. Top with ½ cup chocolate chips. Bake at 300 degrees for 55 minutes or until center is set. Let stand until cool. Chill until serving time.

Yield: 16 servings.   **Prep Time:** 15 minutes plus baking.

CHOCOLATE RIBBON CHEESECAKE

1 cup finely chopped walnuts
1 cup graham cracker crumbs   ¼ cup sugar
½ cup melted margarine   ⅓ cup baking cocoa
24 ounces cream cheese, softened
1   14-ounce can sweetened condensed milk
3 eggs   1 tablespoon vanilla extract

Mix walnuts, crumbs, sugar and ¼ cup margarine in bowl. Press over bottom and 2 inches up side of 9-inch springform pan. Mix ¼ cup butter and cocoa in bowl. Beat cream cheese in bowl until fluffy. Add condensed milk gradually, beating until smooth. Beat in eggs and vanilla. Reserve 1½ cups batter. Add chocolate mixture to remaining batter; mix well. Layer batters ½ at a time in prepared pan; swirl with knife. Bake at 300 degrees for 65 minutes or until set. Let stand for 30 minutes. Loosen side of pan. Cool. Chill overnight. Remove rim of pan; place on serving plate. Garnish with whole walnuts and chocolate curls if desired.

Yield: 16 servings.   **Prep Time:** 20 minutes plus baking.

CHOCOLATE TURTLE CHEESECAKE

2 cups vanilla wafer crumbs
6 tablespoons melted margarine
1   14-ounce package caramels
1   5-ounce can evaporated milk
1 cup chopped pecans, toasted
16 ounces cream cheese, softened   ½ cup sugar
1 teaspoon vanilla extract   2 eggs
½ cup semisweet chocolate chips, melted

Mix wafer crumbs and margarine in bowl. Press over bottom and side of greased 9-inch springform pan. Melt caramels with evaporated milk in saucepan, stirring occasionally. Pour over crust. Sprinkle with pecans. Combine cream cheese, sugar and vanilla in mixer bowl; mix well. Beat in eggs 1 at a time. Beat in chocolate. Pour over caramel layer. Bake at 350 degrees for 40 minutes. Loosen rim. Cool for several minutes. Remove rim. Chill until serving time. Garnish with whipped cream, chopped pecans and maraschino cherries.

Yield: 15 servings.   **Prep Time:** 20 minutes plus baking.

FUDGE TRUFFLE CHEESECAKE

½ cup confectioners' sugar   1½ cups vanilla wafer crumbs
⅓ cup baking cocoa   ⅓ cup melted margarine
24 ounces cream cheese, softened
2 cups semisweet chocolate chips, melted
1   14-ounce can sweetened condensed milk
4 eggs   2 teaspoons vanilla extract

Mix first 4 ingredients in bowl. Press over bottom of 9-inch springform pan. Beat cream cheese in mixer bowl until smooth. Add melted chocolate, condensed milk, eggs and vanilla; mix well. Spoon into prepared pan. Bake at 300 degrees for 1 hour and 5 minutes or until set. Cool to room temperature. Place on serving plate; remove side of pan. Chill until serving time.

Yield: 15 servings.   **Prep Time:** 15 minutes plus baking.

PUMPKIN-ORANGE CHEESECAKE

32 gingersnaps, crushed   1/4 cup melted margarine
24 ounces cream cheese, softened
1 3/4 cups canned pumpkin pie filling
2 eggs   Pumpkin pie spice to taste
1   14-ounce can sweetened condensed milk
3 tablespoons orange juice   1 cup whipped topping

Mix gingersnap crumbs and margarine in bowl. Press over bottom of 9-inch springform pan. Beat cream cheese in mixer bowl until smooth. Add pie filling, eggs, spice, condensed milk and orange juice; mix well. Spoon into prepared pan. Bake at 300 degrees for 1 to 1 1/4 hours or until set. Center will be slightly soft. Let stand at room temperature until cool. Chill overnight. Place on serving plate; remove side of pan. Serve with whipped topping.

Yield: 12 servings.   **Prep Time:** 15 minutes plus baking.

SOUR CREAM CHEESECAKE

1 1/2 cups graham cracker crumbs
1/4 cup sugar   1/2 cup margarine, softened
24 ounces cream cheese, softened
1 1/2 cups sugar   1/8 teaspoon salt
4 eggs   1 teaspoon vanilla extract
8 ounces sour cream   1/4 cup sugar
1 teaspoon vanilla extract

Mix graham cracker crumbs, 1/4 cup sugar and margarine in bowl. Press over bottom and side of 9-inch springform pan. Beat cream cheese, 1 1/2 cups sugar and salt in mixer bowl until light. Add eggs 1 at a time, mixing well after each addition. Add 1 teaspoon vanilla; mix well. Spoon into prepared pan. Bake at 350 degrees for 15 minutes. Increase temperature to 450 degrees. Spread mixture of sour cream, remaining 1/4 cup sugar and 1 teaspoon vanilla over cheesecake. Bake for 10 minutes. Cool. Chill until serving time.

Yield: 16 servings.   **Prep Time:** 15 minutes plus baking.

CHERRIES IN THE SNOW

6 egg whites
1/2 teaspoon cream of tartar
1 1/2 cups sugar
1 cup chopped walnuts
12 saltine crackers, crushed
2 cups whipped topping
1   21-ounce can cherry pie filling

Beat egg whites in mixer bowl until soft peaks form. Add cream of tartar. Add sugar gradually, beating until stiff peaks form. Fold in walnuts and cracker crumbs gently. Place in greased 9x13-inch baking dish. Bake at 350 degrees for 20 minutes. This will rise high and then fall when removed from oven. Let stand until cool. Spread whipped topping over baked layer. Drop pie filling over whipped topping like "cherries falling in the snow." Cut into servings.

Yield: 15 servings.   **Prep Time:** 15 minutes plus baking.

CHERRY DUMP CAKE

1   21-ounce can cherry pie filling
1   8-ounce can crushed pineapple
1   2-layer package yellow cake mix
1/2 cup melted margarine
1/2 cup coconut
1/2 cup chopped pecans

Layer cherry pie filling, pineapple with juice and dry cake mix in 9x13-inch baking dish. Drizzle with margarine. Sprinkle coconut and pecans over top. Bake at 325 degrees for 1 hour.

Yield: 12 servings.   **Prep Time:** 5 minutes plus baking.

*Invest in reusable canvas bags for your grocery shopping
and save both plastic and paper.*

CHERRY YUM-YUM

3 cups graham cracker crumbs
¾ cup melted margarine
8 ounces cream cheese, softened
¾ cup sugar   1 cup cold milk
2 envelopes whipped topping mix
2 21-ounce cans cherry pie filling

Combine crumbs and melted margarine in bowl; mix well. Spread half the mixture in 9x13-inch serving dish. Beat cream cheese and sugar in mixer bowl until light and fluffy. Add milk and whipped topping mix. Beat until stiff. Spoon into prepared dish. Spread with pie filling. Top with remaining crumb mixture. Chill for 24 hours.

Yield: 15 servings.   **Prep Time:** 10 minutes plus chilling.

CHOCOLATE DREAM DESSERT

1 cup flour
½ cup margarine, softened
1 cup chopped pecans
1 cup confectioners' sugar
8 ounces cream cheese, softened
1 cup whipped topping
1 4-ounce package vanilla instant pudding mix
1 4-ounce package chocolate instant pudding mix
2 cups milk
1 8-ounce English toffee candy bar, grated

Combine flour, margarine and pecans in bowl; mix well. Press into 9x13-inch baking dish with fork. Bake at 350 degrees for 20 minutes. Cream confectioners' sugar, cream cheese and whipped topping in mixer bowl until light and fluffy. Spread over cooled crust. Combine pudding mixes and milk in bowl; mix well. Spread over cream cheese mixture. Sprinkle with grated candy. May substitute butterscotch pudding mix for either vanilla or chocolate pudding mix.

Yield: 15 servings.   **Prep Time:** 10 minutes plus baking.

CHOCOLATE RICE

3 cups cooked rice
1 tablespoon baking cocoa
½ cup sugar
1 teaspoon vanilla extract

Place hot cooked rice in large bowl. Stir in cocoa, sugar and vanilla. Spoon into serving dishes. May serve hot or cold.

Yield: 6 servings.　　　　　**Prep Time:** 5 minutes.

BLACKBERRY COBBLER

2 pounds blackberries
⅔ cup packed brown sugar
1 teaspoon cinnamon
1   16-ounce package nut bread mix
2 egg whites

Spread blackberries in 9x11-inch baking dish sprayed with nonstick cooking spray. Sprinkle with brown sugar and cinnamon. Prepare nut bread mix using package directions, substituting egg whites for whole egg and omitting oil. Pour over blackberries. Bake at 400 degrees for 1 hour and 5 minutes or until toothpick inserted in center comes out clean. May substitute other berries for blackberries.

Yield: 12 servings.　　　**Prep Time:** 10 minutes plus baking.

Whenever possible, buy returnable bottles and cans—and then return them. Each bottle can be reused as many as forty or fifty times.

Fruit Cobbler

½ cup melted margarine
1 egg, beaten
1 tablespoon flour
1 cup sugar
4 cups fresh fruit
6 slices white bread, crusts trimmed

Combine margarine and egg in bowl; mix well. Add mixture of flour and sugar. Place fruit in greased 7x11-inch baking dish. Cut bread into finger-sized slices. Arrange lattice-fashion over fruit. Pour butter mixture over top. Bake at 350 degrees for 35 minutes or until golden brown.

Yield: 8 servings.   **Prep Time:** 15 minutes plus baking.

Peach Cobbler

2 cups sliced peaches
1 cup sugar   ½ cup margarine
¾ cup flour   ½ cup sugar
2 teaspoons baking powder
Salt to taste
¾ cup milk

Mix peaches with 1 cup sugar in bowl; set aside. Melt margarine in deep 2-quart baking dish in 350-degree oven. Mix flour, ½ cup sugar, baking powder, salt and milk in bowl. Spoon into prepared baking dish; do not mix. Spoon peaches over batter; do not mix. Bake at 350 degrees for 1 hour or until batter rises to top to form crisp brown crust. Serve with ice cream.

Yield: 6 servings.   **Prep Time:** 10 minutes plus baking.

Sweet Potato Cobbler

4 large sweet potatoes, peeled, thinly sliced
4 cups sugar
2 teaspoons flour
Cinnamon to taste
1 teaspoon vanilla nut flavoring
1 cup margarine
2¹/₂ all-ready pie crusts

Arrange sweet potatoes in 9x13-inch baking pan. Sprinkle with sugar, flour, cinnamon and flavoring. Add a small amount of water to pan. Shake pan to mix slightly. Dot with margarine. Fit pastry over top, sealing edges. Bake at 350 degrees for 20 to 25 minutes or until crust is brown.

Yield: 16 servings.   **Prep Time:** 10 minutes plus baking.

Yummy Coconut Dessert

¹/₂ cup melted margarine
1   7-ounce can coconut
1   2-ounce package slivered almonds
1 cup flour
3 cups milk
2   3-ounce packages vanilla instant pudding mix
12 ounces whipped topping

Combine margarine, coconut, almonds and flour in bowl; mix well. Spread on baking sheet. Bake at 350 degrees for 15 to 20 minutes, stirring every 5 minutes. Cool. Sprinkle ³/₄ of the crumbs in 9x13-inch dish. Mix milk and pudding mix in bowl. Fold in whipped topping. Spoon into prepared dish. Sprinkle with remaining crumbs. Chill in refrigerator.

Yield: 20 servings.   **Prep Time:** 25 minutes.

CRANBERRY MOUSSE

1½ cups whipping cream
12 ounces soft cream cheese
2 tablespoons orange juice
1½ tablespoons sugar
1½ 12-ounce jars cranberry-orange sauce
Fresh cranberries
Mint leaves

Beat whipping cream in mixer bowl until soft peaks form. Combine cream cheese, orange juice and sugar in mixer bowl. Beat until light and fluffy. Stir in cranberry-orange sauce. Fold in whipped cream gently. Spoon mixture into stemmed dessert glasses. Chill until serving time. Garnish with fresh cranberries and mint leaves.

Yield: 6 servings.   **Prep Time:** 10 minutes plus chilling.

DATE NUT ROLL

1 1-pound package graham crackers
1 cup chopped dates
½ cup chopped pecans
1 8-ounce package miniature marshmallows
¼ cup milk

Roll ¼ of the graham crackers between waxed paper into fine crumbs. Crumble remaining crackers into bowl. Add dates, pecans, marshmallows and milk; mix well. Mixture will be sticky. Place mixture on waxed paper sprinkled with fine crumbs. Shape into log. Wrap with waxed paper; twist ends. Roll in towel. Store in refrigerator or freezer. Serve with whipped cream.

Yield: 15 servings.   **Prep Time:** 10 minutes plus chilling.

ÉCLAIR DESSERT

2   4-ounce packages French vanilla instant pudding mix
3 cups milk
9 ounces whipped topping
1   16-ounce package graham crackers
1½ cups confectioners' sugar
2 ounces unsweetened chocolate, melted
2 tablespoons light corn syrup
2 tablespoons margarine
3 tablespoons milk
1 teaspoon vanilla extract

Combine pudding mix and 3 cups milk in bowl; mix until thickened and smooth. Fold in whipped topping. Arrange ⅓ of the graham crackers in 9x13-inch dish. Layer pudding and remaining crackers ½ at a time in dish. Combine confectioners' sugar, chocolate, corn syrup, margarine, 3 tablespoons milk and vanilla in bowl; mix until smooth. Spread over top layer of crackers. Chill for 8 hours to overnight.

Yield: 12 servings.   **Prep Time:** 10 minutes plus chilling.

MANDARIN ORANGE DESSERT

60 butter crackers, crushed
¼ cup sugar
½ cup melted margarine
8 ounces whipped topping
1   14-ounce can sweetened condensed milk
1   6-ounce can frozen orange juice concentrate, thawed
2   11-ounce cans mandarin oranges, drained

Combine cracker crumbs, sugar and melted margarine in bowl; mix well. Press into 9x13-inch glass dish. Combine whipped topping, condensed milk and orange juice concentrate in bowl; mix well. Fold in mandarin oranges. Pour over cracker crust. Chill for 2 hours or longer.

Yield: 16 servings.   **Prep Time:** 10 minutes plus chilling.

HOLIDAY CROWN DESSERT

2 3-ounce packages ladyfingers
2 teaspoons unflavored gelatin
¼ cup cold pineapple juice
¼ cup boiling pineapple juice
½ cup sugar
16 ounces cream cheese, softened
12 ounces whipped topping
1 15-ounce can crushed pineapple, drained

Arrange ladyfingers over bottom and vertically around side of 8-inch springform pan. Soften gelatin in cold juice in bowl. Add boiling juice, stirring until gelatin dissolves. Cream sugar and cream cheese in mixer bowl until light and fluffy. Add gelatin mixture; mix well. Fold in whipped topping and pineapple. Pour into prepared pan. Chill overnight. Remove side of pan. Place on serving plate. Tie wide plaid ribbon around dessert.

Yield: 8 servings.   **Prep Time:** 15 minutes plus chilling.

LEMON DESSERT

1 cup crushed graham crackers
⅓ cup melted margarine
1 6-ounce package frozen lemonade concentrate, thawed
1 14-ounce can sweetened condensed milk
16 ounces whipped topping

Combine graham cracker crumbs and margarine in bowl; mix well. Press into 9x13-inch baking dish. Bake at 325 degrees for 5 minutes. Cool to room temperature. Combine lemonade concentrate and condensed milk in bowl; mix well. Fold in whipped topping. Spoon onto cooled crust. Chill until serving time.

Yield: 12 servings.   **Prep Time:** 15 minutes plus chilling.

PEACH CRUMBLE

1   29-ounce can peaches, drained
2 tablespoons lemon juice
1/4 teaspoon cinnamon
1 tablespoon margarine
1/4 cup melted shortening
1/3 cup packed brown sugar
1/3 cup flour
1/4 teaspoon baking soda
2/3 cup oats
1/2 teaspoon vanilla extract

Arrange peaches in greased baking dish. Sprinkle with lemon juice. Combine cinnamon, margarine, shortening, brown sugar, flour, baking soda, oats and vanilla in bowl; mix until crumbly. Sprinkle over peaches. Bake at 350 degrees for 45 minutes. Serve with whipped cream.

Yield: 4 servings.   **Prep Time:** 5 minutes plus baking.

PEACH MERINGUE WITH RASPBERRIES

4 fresh peaches, peeled, cut into halves
3 egg whites
1 tablespoon honey, warmed
2   10-ounce packages frozen unsweetened raspberries, thawed

Place peaches cut side up in greased shallow baking dish. Beat egg whites until soft peaks form. Add honey gradually, beating until stiff peaks form. Spoon meringue into center of each peach. Bake at 450 degrees for 4 to 5 minutes or until light brown. Spread thawed raspberries in large flat serving dish. Arrange peach halves in raspberries. May substitute one 29-ounce can peaches, drained, for fresh peaches.

Yield: 8 servings.   **Prep Time:** 15 minutes.

CARAMEL PEARS

1   **29-ounce can pear halves, well drained**
3 tablespoons sugar
2 tablespoons margarine
½ cup whipping cream
½ teaspoon vanilla extract

Preheat broiler. Place rack 4 inches from heat source. Arrange pears cut side down in 8x8-inch baking pan. Sprinkle with sugar; dot with margarine. Broil for 8 to 10 minutes, rotating pan if necessary for even browning. Reduce oven temperature to 375 degrees. Pour mixture of whipping cream and vanilla over pears. Bake for 15 minutes or until sauce is brown and bubbly. May substitute apples for pears.

Yield: 6 servings.   **Prep Time:** 5 minutes plus baking.

PINEAPPLE DELIGHT

8 ounces cream cheese, softened
1   **14-ounce can sweetened condensed milk**
16 ounces whipped topping
1 cup miniature marshmallows
1   **8-ounce can pineapple tidbits**

Whip cream cheese and condensed milk in mixer bowl until smooth. Stir in whipped topping, marshmallows and pineapple. Pour into serving dish. Chill in refrigerator.

Yield: 8 servings.   **Prep Time:** 5 minutes plus chilling.

Use juice-pack fruits such as pineapple or peaches
to save calories and carbohydrates.

BANANA AND BERRY BROWNIE PIZZA

1 family-size package brownie mix
8 ounces cream cheese, softened
1 egg   1 teaspoon vanilla extract
1 or 2 bananas, cut into ¼-inch slices
1 pint strawberries, sliced
2 ounces semisweet chocolate
1   14-ounce can sweetened condensed milk

Prepare brownie mix using package directions. Spread batter on greased pizza pan. Bake at 350 degrees for 15 minutes. Beat cream cheese, egg and vanilla at medium speed in mixer bowl until smooth. Spread over crust, leaving ½-inch to 1-inch space around edge. Bake for 15 minutes longer. Cool to room temperature. Arrange bananas and strawberries on top. Microwave chocolate and condensed milk in glass bowl until chocolate is melted, stirring occasionally. Microwave for several minutes longer or until thickened, stirring occasionally. Drizzle over fruit.

Yield: 12 servings.   **Prep Time:** 15 minutes plus baking.

AMERICAN FRUIT PIZZA

1   15-ounce package refrigerator pie pastry
8 ounces cream cheese, softened
2 tablespoons lemon juice   ½ cup sugar
½ cup whipping cream   Assorted fresh fruit
¼ cup apricot preserves   1 tablespoon water

Roll pastry sheets into one 12-inch circle on lightly floured surface. Fit into 10-inch pizza pan. Prick bottom and side with fork. Bake at 400 degrees for 9 to 11 minutes or until light brown. Cool. Blend cream cheese, lemon juice and sugar in mixer bowl. Add whipping cream. Beat at high speed until light and fluffy. Spread over baked shell. Chill for several hours. Arrange fruit over filling. Brush with mixture of preserves and water.

Yield: 12 servings.   **Prep Time:** 15 minutes plus chilling.

DELICIOUS BANANA PUDDING

1 14-ounce can sweetened condensed milk
1½ cups cold water
1 4-ounce package vanilla instant pudding mix
2 cups whipped topping
3 medium bananas, sliced
½ cup lemon juice   36 vanilla wafers

Combine condensed milk, cold water and pudding mix in mixer bowl; mix well. Chill in freezer for 5 minutes. Fold in whipped topping. Combine bananas and lemon juice in bowl, stirring gently to coat bananas; drain. Alternate layers of pudding, vanilla wafers and banana slices in 6x8-inch dish until all are used, ending with pudding. Chill until serving time.

Yield: 8 servings.   **Prep Time:** 10 minutes plus chilling.

BROWNIE PUDDING

1 cup flour
½ teaspoon salt
¾ cup sugar
2 tablespoons baking cocoa
½ cup milk   1 teaspoon vanilla extract
2 tablespoons melted margarine
1 egg   1 cup packed brown sugar
¼ cup baking cocoa
1 cup hot water

Combine flour, salt, sugar and 2 tablespoons baking cocoa in mixer bowl. Add milk, vanilla, melted margarine and egg; mix well. Pour into greased 9x9-inch baking pan. Combine brown sugar, ¼ cup baking cocoa and hot water in mixer bowl; mix well. Pour over batter. Bake in preheated 350-degree oven for 30 to 35 minutes.

Yield: 9 servings.   **Prep Time:** 10 minutes plus baking.

CHERRY RICE CUSTARD PUDDING

1 21-ounce can cherry pie filling
2 cups cooked rice
2 cups milk
3 eggs, beaten
1 teaspoon vanilla extract

Layer pie filling and cooked rice in 3-quart baking dish. Scald milk in saucepan. Stir a small amount of hot milk into eggs; stir eggs into hot milk. Cook until thickened, stirring constantly. Stir in vanilla. Pour over layers. Place in larger pan of water. Bake at 350 degrees for 40 to 50 minutes or until set.

Yield: 8 servings.   **Prep Time:** 15 minutes plus baking.

DOUGHNUT HOLE CUSTARD PUDDING

6 doughnut holes
3 eggs
1/3 cup sugar
1/4 teaspoon salt
1/4 teaspoon nutmeg
1 3/4 cups milk
1 teaspoon vanilla extract

Cut doughnut holes into halves. Arrange in 1 1/2-quart baking dish. Combine eggs and sugar in mixer bowl; mix well. Add salt, nutmeg, milk and vanilla; beat well. Pour over doughnut holes. Bake at 450 degrees for 20 minutes or until knife inserted near center comes out clean. Doughnut holes will rise to top while baking.

Yield: 6 servings.   **Prep Time:** 10 minutes plus baking.

OLD-FASHIONED EGG CUSTARD

3 eggs, beaten
3/4 cup sugar
1 cup milk
2 tablespoons melted margarine
1 tablespoon flour
1/2 teaspoon lemon extract
Nutmeg to taste

Combine eggs and sugar in mixer bowl; beat well. Add milk gradually, beating constantly. Add margarine; mix well. Mix a small amount of batter with flour in bowl. Add flour mixture and lemon extract to batter; mix well. Pour into 9-inch baking pan. Sprinkle with nutmeg. Bake at 375 degrees for 45 minutes or until light brown and custard is set. May bake in pie shell if desired.

Yield: 8 servings.   **Prep Time:** 5 minutes plus baking.

EGGNOG RICE PUDDING

1/2 cup uncooked rice
4 cups eggnog
Cinnamon to taste
Nutmeg to taste

Combine rice and eggnog in 2-quart baking dish; mix well. Sprinkle with spices. Bake at 250 degrees for 2 1/2 hours or until bubbly. Serve warm or chill until serving time.

Yield: 8 servings.   **Prep Time:** 5 minutes plus baking.

*Substitute skim milk for milk in almost any
recipe to lower calories and fat.*

FROSTY PUDDING CONES

⅔ cup sweetened condensed milk
2 tablespoons lemon juice
1 cup peach yogurt
6 sugar ice cream cones
6 tablespoons whipped topping

Combine condensed milk and lemon juice in bowl; mix well. Stir in yogurt. Spoon into sugar cones, leaving ½ inch space at top. Place in upright glasses or tall jars. Freeze for 3 hours or until firm. Top with whipped topping.

Yield: 6 servings.   **Prep Time:** 5 minutes plus freezing.

DELICIOUS PUMPKIN DESSERT

½ cup margarine, softened
1 cup flour
1 cup chopped pecans
1   14-ounce can sweetened condensed milk
1 cup canned pumpkin
1   6-ounce package vanilla instant pudding mix
1½ teaspoons pumpkin pie spice
24 ounces whipped topping

Combine margarine, flour and pecans in bowl; mix well. Spread in 9x13-inch baking dish. Bake at 325 degrees for 20 minutes. Cool. Combine condensed milk, pumpkin, pudding mix, pumpkin pie spice and half the whipped topping in bowl; mix well. Pour over baked layer. Spread remaining whipped topping over filling. Chill in refrigerator.

Yield: 12 servings.   **Prep Time:** 15 minutes plus baking.

*Buy nonfat yogurt for all the flavor without
the calories and fat.*

PUMPKIN PIE SQUARES

1 2-layer package yellow cake mix
½ cup melted margarine   1 egg
1 30-ounce can pumpkin pie mix
2 eggs   ⅔ cup milk
¼ cup sugar   1 teaspoon cinnamon
¼ cup margarine, softened

Reserve 1 cup cake mix for topping. Mix remaining cake mix, ½ cup margarine and 1 egg in bowl. Press into bottom of greased 9x13-inch baking pan. Combine pie mix, 2 eggs and milk in mixer bowl; beat until smooth. Pour into prepared pan. Mix reserved cake mix, ¼ cup sugar, cinnamon and ¼ cup margarine in small bowl. Sprinkle over filling. Bake at 350 degrees for 45 to 50 minutes or until knife inserted near center comes out clean. May serve warm or cold with whipped cream. May substitute mixture of 16 ounces pumpkin, 2½ teaspoons pumpkin pie spice and ½ cup packed brown sugar for pumpkin pie mix.

Yield: 12 servings.   **Prep Time:** 10 minutes plus baking.

PUNCH BOWL CAKE

2 6-ounce packages vanilla instant pudding mix
6 cups milk   4 cups white cake pieces
16 ounces whipped topping
1 cup sliced strawberries   1 cup sliced bananas
1 cup seedless grape halves
1 cup pineapple tidbits   1 cup mandarin oranges
½ cup sliced kiwifruit
Red maraschino cherries

Combine pudding mix and milk in bowl; mix well. Alternate layers of cake, whipped topping, fruit and pudding in large glass bowl, ending with whipped topping. Top with additional kiwifruit slices and cherries. Chill in refrigerator.

Yield: 20 servings.   **Prep Time:** 15 minutes plus chilling.

RASPBERRY SWIRL

⅓ cup melted margarine
1 7-ounce package coconut, toasted
2 envelopes unflavored gelatin   ¼ cup water
1 14-ounce can sweetened condensed milk
1 cup sour cream   1 cup whipping cream, whipped
1 10-ounce package frozen raspberries in syrup, thawed
4 teaspoons cornstarch

Combine margarine and coconut in bowl; mix well. Press onto bottom and side of greased 8-inch springform pan. Chill in refrigerator. Sprinkle gelatin in water in saucepan. Let stand for 1 minute. Cook over low heat until gelatin is dissolved, stirring constantly. Combine condensed milk, sour cream and gelatin in mixer bowl; mix well. Fold in whipped cream. Chill, covered, for 30 minutes or until partially set. Purée raspberries in blender. Combine raspberries and cornstarch in saucepan; mix well. Cook until thick and glossy, stirring constantly. Cool to room temperature. Layer gelatin mixture and raspberries ½ at a time over coconut crust. Swirl gently with knife. Chill for 4 hours or until set. Remove side of springform pan.

Yield: 10 servings.   **Prep Time:** 20 minutes plus chilling

RITZ CRACKER DESSERT

4 egg whites   1 cup sugar
1 teaspoon vanilla extract   40 Ritz crackers, crushed
1 cup chopped pecans   2 cups whipping cream, whipped
2 cups miniature marshmallows   ½ cup coconut

Beat egg whites in mixer bowl until soft peaks form. Add sugar gradually, beating until stiff peaks form. Add vanilla, cracker crumbs and pecans; mix well. Spoon into greased 9x13-inch baking dish. Bake at 325 degrees for 25 minutes. Cool. Spread whipped cream over cooled dessert. Sprinkle with marshmallows and coconut. Chill until serving time. May store for several days in refrigerator.

Yield: 12 servings.   **Prep Time:** 15 minutes plus baking.

DANISH APPLESAUCE TORTE

2 cups thick applesauce
1½ cups ground almonds
1½ tablespoons confectioners' sugar
3 egg yolks
3 egg whites

Spread applesauce in buttered 9x13-inch baking dish. Mix almonds and confectioners' sugar in mixer bowl. Beat in egg yolks 1 at a time. Beat egg whites in mixer bowl until stiff peaks form. Fold into egg yolk mixture. Spoon evenly over applesauce. Bake at 400 degrees for 1 hour.

Yield: 15 servings.　　**Prep Time:** 10 minutes plus baking.

MAKE-AHEAD MOCHA CREAM TORTE

1 pint whipping cream
1 cup confectioners' sugar
3 tablespoons chocolate syrup
2 teaspoons instant coffee
1　16-ounce package graham crackers
½ cup shaved chocolate

Beat whipping cream in large mixer bowl until soft peaks form. Add confectioners' sugar, chocolate syrup and coffee granules. Layer graham crackers and mocha cream ⅓ at a time in 9x13-inch dish. Chill in refrigerator. Garnish with shaved chocolate.

Yield: 16 servings.　　**Prep Time:** 10 minutes plus chilling.

*Whipped chilled evaporated milk and whipped topping mix
are lower in fat and calories than whipped cream.*

FANTASTIC CHOCOLATE TRIFLE

1   6-ounce package chocolate instant pudding mix
½ cup strong coffee
½ cup chocolate syrup
1   1-pound chocolate cake, cut into small pieces
1   12-ounce package brickle chips
or crushed English toffee
2 cups whipping cream, whipped
1   7-ounce package slivered almonds
12 maraschino cherries

Prepare pudding mix using package directions. Mix coffee and chocolate syrup in bowl. Layer cake, chocolate mixture, brickle, pudding and whipped cream ½ at a time in trifle dish or transparent glass bowl. Top with almonds and cherries.

Yield: 12 servings.   **Prep Time:** 15 minutes plus chilling.

LIGHT STRAWBERRY TRIFLE

2 angel food cakes, cut into small pieces
1   12-ounce jar strawberry nectar
9 cups nonfat strawberry yogurt
16 cups sliced strawberries

Layer cake, strawberry nectar, yogurt and strawberries ¼ at a time in 5-quart glass bowl. Chill for 4 hours to overnight. May substitute other fruits and nectars.

Yield: 20 servings.   **Prep Time:** 10 minutes plus chilling.

*Angel food cake is delicious by itself or as an ingredient
in other desserts and contains no fat or cholesterol.*

FANTASTIC PIES

Nutritional information for Fantastic Pies is on page 160.

MICROWAVE APPLE PIE

1 cup sour cream
¾ cup sugar   ¼ teaspoon salt
1 teaspoon vanilla extract
1 egg
2 tablespoons flour
4 cups sliced apples
1 baked 9-inch pie shell
½ cup packed brown sugar
5 tablespoons flour
3 tablespoons margarine

Combine sour cream, sugar, salt, vanilla, egg and 2 tablespoons flour in mixer bowl. Beat until well blended. Fold in apples. Pour into pie shell. Microwave on Medium for 5 minutes. Stir in filling gently. Microwave on Low for 10 to 12 minutes or until set. Mix brown sugar and 5 tablespoons flour in bowl. Cut in margarine until crumbly. Sprinkle over pie. Microwave on Low for 8 to 10 minutes or until bubbly. Cool on wire rack.

Yield: 8 servings.   **Prep Time:** 10 minutes plus cooking.

AVOCADO PIE

2 large ripe avocados, chopped
1 cup sweetened condensed milk
Juice of 2 limes
1½ cups chopped walnuts
1 teaspoon nutmeg
1   9-inch graham cracker pie shell

Combine avocados, condensed milk, lime juice, walnuts and nutmeg in blender container. Process until smooth. Pour into pie shell. Chill for 2 hours.

Yield: 8 servings.   **Prep Time:** 5 minutes plus chilling.

BANANA CREAM PIE

1 cup sugar
3 tablespoons flour
3 eggs
1½ cups milk
Salt to taste
1 teaspoon vanilla extract
2 bananas, chopped
1 baked 9-inch pie shell

Combine sugar, flour and eggs in saucepan. Stir in milk, salt and vanilla. Cook until thickened, stirring constantly. Cool to room temperature. Stir in bananas. Spoon into pie shell. Chill until serving time. Garnish with whipped cream.

Yield: 8 servings.   **Prep Time:** 20 minutes plus chilling.

BLACK RUSSIAN PIE

14 Oreo cookies, crushed
2 tablespoons melted butter
24 marshmallows
Salt to taste
½ cup milk
2 tablespoons chocolate syrup
3 tablespoons strong coffee
1 cup whipping cream, whipped

Combine cookie crumbs and butter in 8-inch pie plate; mix well. Press over bottom and side of pie plate. Freeze until firm. Melt marshmallows with salt and milk in double boiler. Cool until partially set. Stir in mixture of chocolate syrup and coffee. Fold in whipped cream gently. Pour into prepared pie plate. Freeze until firm. Garnish with chocolate curls.

Yield: 8 servings.   **Prep Time:** 20 minutes plus freezing.

FRESH BLUEBERRY PIE

3 cups fresh blueberries
1 baked 9-inch pie shell
1/2 cup sugar
2 tablespoons cornstarch
1 cup water
1 cup whipping cream
1/4 cup sugar

Place 2 cups blueberries in pie shell. Place 1 cup blueberries in blender container. Process until smooth. Combine with 1/2 cup sugar, cornstarch and water in saucepan. Cook until thickened, stirring constantly. Cool slightly. Pour over blueberries in pie shell. Chill until serving time. Whip cream with 1/4 cup sugar in bowl until soft peaks form. Cut pie into wedges. Top with whipped cream.

Yield: 8 servings.   **Prep Time:** 15 minutes plus chilling.

BUTTERSCOTCH PIE

1/3 cup sifted flour
1 cup packed brown sugar
1/4 teaspoon salt
3 egg yolks, beaten
1/4 cup margarine
1/2 teaspoon vanilla extract
2 cups milk, scalded
1 baked 8-inch pie shell

Combine flour, brown sugar, salt, egg yolks, margarine and vanilla in saucepan; mix well. Stir in milk very gradually. Cook until thickened, stirring constantly. Pour into pie shell. Chill until serving time.

Yield: 8 servings.   **Prep Time:** 10 minutes plus chilling.

CARAMEL PIES

1   24-ounce package caramels
½ cup water
1 cup sour cream
16 ounces whipped topping
2   9-inch butter cookie crumb pie shells

Cook caramels and water in saucepan over low heat until caramels are melted, stirring constantly. Let stand until cool. Fold in sour cream and whipped topping. Spoon into pie shells. Chill until serving time.

Yield: 12 servings.   **Prep Time:** 15 minutes plus chilling.

CHERRY CREAM CHEESE PIE

8 ounces cream cheese, softened
1   14-ounce can sweetened condensed milk
⅓ cup lemon juice
1 teaspoon vanilla extract
1 graham cracker pie shell
1   21-ounce can cherry pie filling

Beat cream cheese in mixer bowl until light. Add condensed milk gradually, beating until smooth. Stir in lemon juice and vanilla. Spoon into pie shell. Chill until serving time. Top with pie filling.

Yield: 8 servings.   **Prep Time:** 10 minutes plus chilling.

*Graham cracker or cookie crumb pie shells have far
fewer calories from fat than pie pastry.*

CHESS TARTS

1/2 cup margarine, softened
4 cups packed brown sugar
5 eggs, beaten
3 tablespoons milk
1 1/2 teaspoons vanilla extract
36 unbaked tart shells

Cream margarine and brown sugar in mixer bowl until light and fluffy. Beat in eggs, milk and vanilla. Spoon into tart shells. Bake at 350 degrees for 10 to 15 minutes or until set. May reduce recipe by half, reducing eggs from 5 to 3.

Yield: 36 servings.   **Prep Time:** 5 minutes plus baking.

CHOCOLATE CHESS PIE

1 cup sugar
2 eggs, beaten
Salt to taste
1 teaspoon vanilla extract
1/2 cup margarine
1 ounce unsweetened chocolate
1 unbaked 9-inch pie shell

Combine sugar, eggs, salt and vanilla in bowl; mix well. Melt margarine and chocolate in saucepan, stirring frequently. Add to sugar mixture; mix well. Pour into pie shell. Bake at 350 degrees for 25 to 30 minutes or until set. Garnish with whipped cream.

Yield: 8 servings.   **Prep Time:** 10 minutes plus baking.

CHOCOLATE RASPBERRY TARTS

8 ounces cream cheese, softened
8 ounces semisweet chocolate chips, melted
2 tablespoons raspberry syrup
4 graham cracker tart shells
1 cup raspberries

Combine cream cheese, melted chocolate and raspberry syrup in bowl; mix well. Spoon into tart shells. Top with raspberries. Garnish with mint sprigs. Chill in refrigerator until serving time.

Yield: 4 servings.   **Prep Time:** 5 minutes plus chilling.

CHOCOLATE TRUFFLE PIE

1 envelope unflavored gelatin
1/3 cup orange juice, chilled
1 cup semisweet chocolate chips
1 teaspoon vanilla extract
2 eggs, slightly beaten
1/4 cup sugar
1 1/2 cups whipping cream, whipped
1   9-inch chocolate crumb pie shell

Soften gelatin in orange juice in medium saucepan for 1 minute. Cook over low heat until gelatin is dissolved, stirring constantly. Add chocolate. Cook until chocolate is melted, stirring frequently. Stir in vanilla. Let stand for 10 minutes or until lukewarm. Beat eggs and sugar at high speed in mixer bowl for 5 minutes or until light and fluffy. Stir in chocolate mixture. Fold in whipped cream. Pour into pie shell. Chill until set. Garnish with chocolate shavings.

Yield: 8 servings.   **Prep Time:** 20 minutes plus chilling.

MICROWAVE COCONUT PIE

4 egg yolks   1 cup sugar
3 tablespoons (heaping) cornstarch
2 cups milk   1½ teaspoons vanilla extract
½ cup margarine   1 7-ounce can flaked coconut
1 baked 9-inch deep-dish pie shell
4 egg whites   ¼ cup sugar

Beat egg yolks in glass bowl. Add 1 cup sugar; mix well. Stir in cornstarch, milk and vanilla. Microwave on High for 8 minutes, stirring every 2 minutes. Stir in margarine until melted. Reserve a small amount of coconut for topping. Add remaining coconut to egg mixture; mix well. Pour into pie shell. Beat egg whites in mixer bowl until soft peaks form. Add ¼ cup sugar gradually, beating until stiff peaks form. Spread over pie, sealing to edge. Sprinkle with reserved coconut. Bake at 400 degrees until brown.

Yield: 8 servings.   **Prep Time:** 10 minutes plus baking.

COCONUT CREAM PIE

¾ cup sugar   ¼ cup cornstarch
Salt to taste   2 cups milk, scalded
3 egg yolks   ¾ cup coconut
2 tablespoons margarine, softened
1 teaspoon vanilla extract
1 baked 9-inch pie shell
8 ounces whipped topping

Mix sugar, cornstarch and salt in saucepan. Stir in milk. Cook until thickened, stirring constantly. Add egg yolks 1 at a time, mixing well after each addition. Cook for 10 minutes longer, stirring frequently. Stir in coconut, margarine and vanilla. Cool slightly. Pour into pie shell. Spread whipped topping over top. May substitute sliced bananas or other fruit for coconut.

Yield: 6 servings.   **Prep Time:** 20 minutes.

COFFEE-ALMOND PIE

2 envelopes unflavored gelatin
1/2 cup cold water   2 cups double-strength coffee
2/3 cup sugar   1/2 teaspoon nutmeg
3 egg yolks, beaten
8 ounces whipping cream, whipped
3 egg whites, stiffly beaten   1 cup chopped almonds
1½ teaspoons vanilla extract   1 baked 10-inch pie shell

Soften gelatin in cold water. Blend coffee, sugar and nutmeg in double boiler. Bring to a boil over hot water, stirring until sugar dissolves. Stir a small amount of hot mixture into beaten egg yolks; stir egg yolks into hot mixture. Cook until thickened, stirring constantly. Remove from heat. Add gelatin; stir until dissolved. Chill until partially set. Fold in whipped cream, egg whites, almonds and vanilla. Spoon into pie shell. Chill until set. Garnish with chocolate curls.

Yield: 8 servings.   **Prep Time:** 15 minutes plus chilling.

CRANBERRY MINCE PIE

1 jar mincemeat   1 recipe 2-crust pie pastry
2/3 cup sugar   2 tablespoons cornstarch
2/3 cup water
1½ cups fresh cranberries
2 tablespoons milk   1 tablespoon sugar

Spoon mincemeat into pastry-lined pie plate. Combine 2/3 cup sugar, cornstarch and water in saucepan; mix well. Bring to a boil over high heat, stirring frequently. Stir in cranberries. Return to a boil. Simmer over low heat for 5 to 10 minutes or until thickened, stirring occasionally. Pour over mincemeat. Top with remaining pastry. Seal and flute edge; cut vents. Brush with milk; sprinkle with 1 tablespoon sugar. Bake at 425 degrees for 30 minutes.

Yield: 8 servings.   **Prep Time:** 20 minutes plus baking.

EGGNOG CHIFFON PIE

1 envelope unflavored gelatin
¼ cup milk   3 egg yolks
¼ cup sugar   1½ cups eggnog
1 teaspoon brandy extract
½ teaspoon vanilla extract
3 egg whites   ¼ cup sugar
1 baked 9-inch pie shell

Soften gelatin in milk in small bowl. Beat egg yolks and ¼ cup sugar in bowl. Heat eggnog in double boiler over boiling water. Stir a small amount of hot eggnog into egg yolks; stir egg yolks into hot eggnog. Cook over simmering water for 10 to 12 minutes or until thickened, stirring constantly; remove from heat. Stir in gelatin until dissolved. Stir in flavorings. Chill until thickened. Beat egg whites in mixer bowl until foamy. Add ¼ cup sugar gradually, beating until soft peaks form. Fold gently into eggnog mixture. Spoon into pie shell. Chill until serving time.

Yield: 8 servings.   **Prep Time:** 20 minutes plus chilling.

GRAPEFRUIT PIE

1 cup sugar
1¾ cups water
2 tablespoons cornstarch
1   3-ounce package strawberry gelatin
Sections of 3 grapefruit
1 baked 9-inch pie shell

Mix sugar, water and cornstarch in saucepan. Cook over medium heat until thickened and clear, stirring frequently. Remove from heat. Add gelatin, stirring until dissolved. Chill until partially set. Fold in grapefruit. Pour into pie shell. Chill until serving time. Garnish with whipped topping.

Yield: 8 servings.   **Prep Time:** 15 minutes plus chilling.

FRENCH SILK PIE

1 cup margarine, softened
6 tablespoons baking cocoa
1 tablespoon vanilla extract
1½ cups sugar
1 cup egg substitute
1 baked 9-inch pie shell
1 cup whipping cream, whipped

Combine margarine, cocoa, vanilla and sugar in large mixer bowl; mix well. Add egg substitute; beat for 5 minutes. Pour into pie shell. Chill until serving time. Top with whipped cream. Garnish with chocolate shavings.

Yield: 8 servings.   **Prep Time:** 15 minutes.

GERMAN MINT PIE

1⅓ cups vanilla wafer crumbs
¼ cup sugar
¼ cup melted margarine
½ cup butter, softened
¾ cup sugar
¾ cup egg substitute
2 ounces unsweetened chocolate, melted
4 ounces German's sweet chocolate, melted
¼ teaspoon peppermint extract

Combine wafer crumbs, ¼ cup sugar and ¼ cup melted margarine in bowl; mix well. Press over bottom and side of 9-inch pie plate. Bake at 375 degrees for 5 minutes. Cream ½ cup butter and ¾ cup sugar in mixer bowl until light and fluffy. Beat in egg substitute. Add mixture of chocolates and peppermint extract; mix well. Pour into prepared pie plate. Chill until serving time.

Yield: 8 servings.   **Prep Time:** 15 minutes plus chilling.

GRASSHOPPER PIE

24 chocolate wafers, finely crushed
1/4 cup melted margarine
2 cups whipped cream
1   7-ounce jar marshmallow creme
1/4 cup non-alcoholic Crème de Menthe

Combine wafer crumbs and margarine in bowl; mix well. Reserve 2 cups crumb mixture. Press remaining crumb mixture over bottom and side of greased 9-inch pie plate. Fold whipped cream and marshmallow creme together in bowl. Fold in Crème de Menthe. Spoon into prepared pie plate. Sprinkle with reserved crumb mixture. Freeze until firm.

Yield: 8 servings.   **Prep Time:** 10 minutes plus freezing.

MICROWAVE HONEY-LEMON PIE

1 cup oats
1/3 cup chopped pecans
2 tablespoons brown sugar
1/2 teaspoon cinnamon
1/4 cup melted margarine
4 1/2 teaspoons unflavored gelatin
1/2 cup water
3 cups lemon yogurt
1/4 cup honey
1 1/2 cups whipping cream, whipped

Mix oats, pecans, brown sugar and cinnamon in bowl. Add margarine; mix well. Press into oiled 9-inch pie plate. Microwave on High for 3 to 4 minutes. Let stand until cool. Soften gelatin in water in glass measure. Microwave on High for 1 to 2 minutes or until dissolved. Blend yogurt and honey in bowl. Add gelatin gradually, beating constantly. Chill until partially set. Fold in whipped cream gently. Spoon into pie shell. Chill until serving time.

Yield: 8 servings.   **Prep Time:** 10 minutes plus chilling.

KIWIFRUIT AND LIME PIES

12 egg yolks, beaten
1½ cups sugar
¾ teaspoon salt
1 cup fresh lime juice
3 cups whipping cream, whipped
3 graham cracker pie shells
6 kiwifruit, peeled, sliced

Combine egg yolks, sugar, salt and lime juice in saucepan. Cook over medium heat until thickened, stirring constantly. Cool. Fold into whipped cream gently. Spoon into pie shells. Chill until serving time. Top with sliced kiwifruit. Garnish with additional whipped cream and twisted lime slices.

Yield: 24 servings.   **Prep Time:** 15 minutes plus chilling.

LEMON PIE

1   14-ounce can sweetened condensed milk
3 egg yolks
½ cup lemon juice
1 graham cracker pie shell
3 egg whites
6 tablespoons sugar

Combine condensed milk, egg yolks and lemon juice in bowl; mix well. Pour into pie shell. Beat egg whites with sugar in mixer bowl until stiff peaks form. Spread over pie, sealing to edge. Bake at 350 degrees for 15 minutes or just until brown. Cool to room temperature. Store in refrigerator.

Yield: 8 servings.   **Prep Time:** 15 minutes plus baking.

Egg substitute contains little fat and no cholesterol and is safer for uncooked desserts than fresh eggs.

SOUR CREAM LEMON PIE

1 cup sugar
3 tablespoons cornstarch
1 tablespoon grated lemon rind
¼ cup lemon juice
½ teaspoon salt
¼ cup margarine, softened
3 egg yolks, slightly beaten
1 cup milk
1 cup sour cream
1 baked 8-inch pie shell
1 cup whipping cream, whipped

Combine sugar, cornstarch, lemon rind, lemon juice, salt, margarine, egg yolks and milk in saucepan. Cook until thickened, stirring constantly. Cool. Add sour cream. Pour into pie shell. Top with whipped cream.

Yield: 8 servings.   **Prep Time:** 15 minutes.

KEY LARGO LIME TART

½ cup margarine
1 cup sugar
1 cup fresh lime juice
4 egg yolks   2 eggs
1 tablespoon grated lime rind
2 drops of green food coloring
1 baked 9-inch pie shell
½ cup coconut, lightly toasted

Melt margarine in saucepan over low heat. Whisk in sugar, lime juice, egg yolks, eggs and lime rind. Cook until thickened, stirring constantly. Stir in food coloring. Cool to room temperature. Spoon into pie shell. Top with toasted coconut. Chill until serving time.

Yield: 8 servings.   **Prep Time:** 15 minutes plus chilling.

LUAU PIE

1 4-ounce package vanilla instant pudding mix
1½ cups sour cream
2 tablespoons sugar
½ cup milk
1 teaspoon grated lime rind
½ teaspoon rum extract
1 8-ounce can crushed pineapple, drained
1 cup coconut
1 baked 9-inch pie shell

Combine pudding mix, sour cream, sugar, milk, lime rind and rum extract in medium bowl. Beat at low speed for 1 minute or until smooth. Fold in pineapple and coconut. Spoon into cooled pie shell. Chill until serving time. Garnish with whipped topping, fruit and mint leaves.

Yield: 8 servings.   **Prep Time:** 5 minutes plus chilling.

MAPLE SYRUP PIE

1 recipe 2-crust pie pastry
1 cup maple syrup
½ cup water
3 tablespoons cornstarch
2 tablespoons cold water
¼ cup chopped walnuts
1 tablespoon margarine

Line 8-inch pie plate with half the pastry. Combine maple syrup and ½ cup water in saucepan. Bring to a boil. Cook for 5 minutes. Add cornstarch blended with 2 tablespoons cold water. Cook until thickened, stirring constantly. Add walnuts and margarine. Pour into prepared pie plate. Top with remaining pastry. Seal edges; cut vents. Bake at 450 degrees for 30 minutes or until golden brown.

Yield: 8 servings.   **Prep Time:** 15 minutes plus baking.

MINCEMEAT CHIFFON PIE

1 envelope unflavored gelatin
1/4 cup cold water
1   16-ounce jar mincemeat
3 egg yolks
1 tablespoon grated orange rind
3 egg whites   1/2 cup sugar
1 cup whipping cream, whipped
1 baked 9-inch pie shell

Soften gelatin in cold water. Combine mincemeat, egg yolks and orange rind in saucepan. Cook over low heat until steaming, stirring constantly. Add gelatin; mix until dissolved. Chill until partially set. Beat egg whites until soft peaks form. Add sugar gradually, beating until stiff. Fold in mincemeat mixture gently. Fold in half the whipped cream. Spoon into pie shell. Chill until serving time. Garnish with remaining whipped cream.

Yield: 8 servings.   **Prep Time:** 25 minutes plus chilling.

NUTTY BUDDY PIES

8 ounces cream cheese, softened
1 cup milk
2 cups confectioners' sugar
2/3 cup chunky peanut butter
16 ounces whipped topping
3   9-inch graham cracker pie shells
3/4 cup chocolate syrup
1 cup chopped salted peanuts

Combine cream cheese and milk in mixer bowl; beat until blended. Add confectioners' sugar, peanut butter and whipped topping; mix well. Spoon into pie shells. Drizzle with chocolate syrup; sprinkle with peanuts. Freeze until serving time.

Yield: 24 servings.   **Prep Time:** 10 minutes plus freezing.

ORANGE-LIME PIES

1 envelope unflavored gelatin
2/3 cup orange juice
8 egg yolks, slightly beaten
2 tablespoons grated orange rind
2/3 cup sugar   1/2 cup lime juice
8 egg whites   1/2 teaspoon salt
1 cup sugar   2 baked 9-inch pie shells

Soften gelatin in orange juice in bowl. Combine egg yolks, orange rind, 2/3 cup sugar and lime juice in double boiler, stir until smooth. Cook over boiling water until thickened, stirring constantly. Add gelatin mixture; mix to dissolve well. Remove from heat. Beat egg whites and salt in mixer bowl until soft peaks form. Add 1 cup sugar gradually, beating until stiff peaks form. Fold gently into orange juice mixture. Pour into pie shells. Chill until serving time.

Yield: 16 servings.   **Prep Time:** 20 minutes plus chilling.

PINEAPPLE PIE

1 cup sugar
3 tablespoons (heaping) flour
1/2 teaspoon salt
2 egg yolks   1/4 cup water
1   8-ounce can crushed pineapple
1 tablespoon shortening
Juice and grated rind of 1 lemon
1 baked pie shell

Combine sugar, flour, salt and egg yolks in bowl; mix well. Bring water and pineapple to a boil in saucepan. Add sugar mixture; mix well. Cook until thickened, stirring constantly. Stir in shortening, lemon juice and lemon rind. Spoon into pie shell. Chill until serving time.

Yield: 8 servings.   **Prep Time:** 15 minutes.

MICROWAVE PEACH-RAISIN PIE

2 16-ounce cans sliced peaches
1/2 cup sugar
2 to 3 tablespoons cornstarch
1/2 cup raisins
1/2 teaspoon nutmeg
1/4 teaspoon cinnamon
1 recipe 2-crust pie pastry
1 tablespoon margarine

Drain peaches, reserving juice of 1 can. Mix sugar, cornstarch and reserved juice in glass dish. Microwave, covered, on High for 2 minutes or until thickened, stirring twice. Mix in peaches, raisins and spices. Pour into pastry-lined 9-inch pie plate. Dot with margarine. Top with remaining pastry; seal edge and cut vents. Microwave on High for 6 minutes or until bubbly, turning twice. Bake at 450 degrees for 10 minutes or until golden.

Yield: 8 servings.   **Prep Time:** 15 minutes plus baking.

PEANUT BUTTER PIE

6 ounces cream cheese, softened
3/4 cup confectioners' sugar
2 tablespoons milk
1/2 cup creamy peanut butter
8 ounces whipped topping
1 graham cracker pie shell

Combine cream cheese, confectioners' sugar, milk and peanut butter in mixer bowl; mix until smooth. Fold in whipped topping. Spoon into pie shell. Chill until serving time. Garnish with crushed peanuts.

Yield: 8 servings.   **Prep Time:** 5 minutes plus chilling.

PECAN CARAMEL TART

36 vanilla caramels
½ cup whipping cream
3½ cups pecan halves
1 baked 9-inch pie shell
1 teaspoon margarine
¼ cup semisweet chocolate chips
1 tablespoon whipping cream

Combine caramels and ½ cup whipping cream in saucepan. Cook over low heat until caramels melt, stirring occasionally. Remove from heat. Add pecan halves; mix well. Spoon into pie shell. Melt margarine and chocolate chips in small saucepan, stirring constantly. Stir in 1 tablespoon whipping cream. Drizzle over pecan filling. Chill until serving time. Garnish with whipped cream.

Yield: 8 servings.   **Prep Time:** 15 minutes plus chilling.

PUMPKIN CHIFFON PIE

1 cup pumpkin
1   11-ounce package marshmallows
1½ teaspoons cinnamon
1½ teaspoons nutmeg
1 teaspoon ground cloves
2 cups whipping cream, whipped
1 baked 9-inch deep-dish pie shell

Combine pumpkin and marshmallows in large saucepan. Cook over medium heat until marshmallows melt, stirring frequently. Stir in cinnamon, nutmeg and cloves; cool. Fold whipped cream into pumpkin mixture gently. Pour into pie shell. Chill until serving time. Garnish with additional whipped cream.

Yield: 8 servings.   **Prep Time:** 15 minutes plus chilling.

MARSHMALLOW AND STRAWBERRY PIE

20 large marshmallows
1/2 cup milk
1 cup whipped topping
1 pint fresh strawberries, sliced
1   8-inch graham cracker pie shell
8 whole strawberries

Melt marshmallows in milk in saucepan over low heat, stirring until smooth. Let stand until cool. Fold in whipped topping and sliced strawberries. Spoon into pie shell. Top with whole strawberries. Chill, covered with plastic wrap, until serving time. May substitute other fresh fruit for strawberries.

Yield: 6 servings.   **Prep Time:** 10 minutes plus chilling.

ZUCCHINI PIE

1 cup sliced peeled zucchini, cooked
1 cup sugar   2 eggs
2 tablespoons flour
1 cup evaporated milk
2 tablespoons margarine
1 teaspoon vanilla extract
1 unbaked 9-inch pie shell
Nutmeg and cinnamon to taste

Combine zucchini, sugar, eggs, flour, evaporated milk, margarine and vanilla in blender container. Process at high speed until mixture is smooth. Pour into unbaked 9-inch pie shell. Sprinkle with nutmeg and cinnamon. Bake at 425 degrees for 10 minutes. Reduce oven temperature to 350 degrees. Bake for 15 minutes longer or until knife inserted near center comes out clean.

Yield: 8 servings.   **Prep Time:** 5 minutes plus baking.

UNBEATABLE BEVERAGES

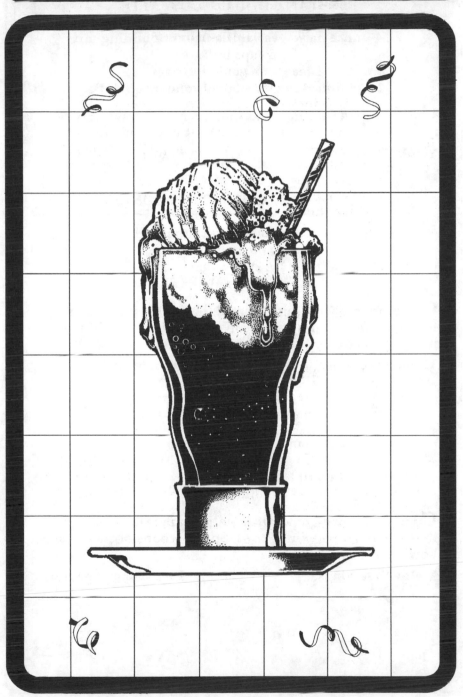

Nutritional information for Unbeatable Beverages is on pages 160–161.

INSTANT BOILED CUSTARD

2   4-ounce packages vanilla instant pudding mix
8 cups milk
1 teaspoon vanilla extract
1   14-ounce can sweetened condensed milk

Combine pudding mix and milk in mixer bowl; mix well. Add vanilla and condensed milk; beat until smooth.

Yield: 20 servings.   **Prep Time:** 5 minutes.

SPARKLING CHRISTMAS PUNCH

4 cups cranberry juice cocktail
4 cups pineapple juice
1½ cups sugar
2 quarts ginger ale, chilled

Combine cranberry juice cocktail, pineapple juice and sugar in pitcher. Stir until sugar dissolves. Chill in refrigerator. Pour into punch bowl. Add ginger ale just before serving.

Yield: 32 servings.   **Prep Time:** 5 minutes plus chilling.

EASTER PUNCH

3 cups orange-grapefruit juice, chilled
3 cups pineapple juice, chilled
1 quart lemon-lime soda, chilled
1 cup lime sherbet

Combine orange-grapefruit juice, pineapple juice and lemon-lime soda in large punch bowl. Spoon scoops of sherbet into bowl. Serve immediately.

Yield: 40 servings.   **Prep Time:** 5 minutes.

FRUIT PUNCH

1   6-ounce can frozen orange juice concentrate
Ice cubes
1   12-ounce can guava nectar

Prepare orange juice using directions on can. Combine with ice cubes and guava nectar in large pitcher; mix well. Pour into serving glasses. Garnish with orange slices.

Yield: 8 servings.   **Prep Time:** 5 minutes.

LEMON-GRAPE PUNCH

1 cup lemon juice
12 cups grape juice
16 cups ginger ale
¼ cup sugar

Mix lemon juice, grape juice and ginger ale in punch bowl. Stir in sugar. Add ice ring if desired. Serve over crushed ice or small scoops of lemon sherbet in punch cups. Use purple, red or white grape juice or mixture in any proportions.

Yield: 30 servings.   **Prep Time:** 5 minutes.

GRAPE JUICE FIZZ

1 quart grape juice, chilled
1 quart lemon-lime soda, chilled

Combine grape juice and lemon-lime soda in large pitcher. Serve immediately.

Yield: 8 servings.   **Prep Time:** 2 minutes.

MERRY BERRY PUNCH

6 cups orange juice
2 cups cranberry juice cocktail
2   10-ounce packages frozen quick-thaw
strawberries in syrup
3 cups ginger ale

Combine orange juice, cranberry juice cocktail and strawberries in large punch bowl. Add ginger ale; mix gently. Add ice cubes if desired.

Yield: 25 servings.   **Prep Time:** 5 minutes.

MEXICAN PUNCH

1 papaya
3 bananas
3 apples, peeled
1 cup sugar
1 teaspoon cinnamon
1 quart ice water

Cut papaya, bananas and apples into chunks. Process with sugar, cinnamon and ice water in blender until smooth and creamy. Pour into glasses.

Yield: 10 servings.   **Prep Time:** 10 minutes.

MOCK PIÑA COLADA PUNCH

1   46-ounce can pineapple juice, chilled
1   16-ounce can cream of coconut, chilled
1   28-ounce bottle of lemon-lime soda, chilled
1 quart vanilla ice cream

Combine pineapple juice, cream of coconut and lemon-lime soda in punch bowl. Add scoops of ice cream.

Yield: 30 servings.   **Prep Time:** 5 minutes.

ORANGE BREAKFAST NOG

1 cup skim milk
¼ cup frozen orange juice concentrate, partially thawed
1 tablespoon sugar
1 teaspoon vanilla extract
4 ice cubes

Combine skim milk, orange juice concentrate, sugar, vanilla and ice cubes in blender container. Process until well blended and frothy. Pour into tall glasses.

Yield: 2 servings.   **Prep Time:** 5 minutes.

PARTY PUNCH

4   46-ounce cans Hawaiian punch, chilled
½ gallon orange sherbet
½ lemon, sliced
½ lime, sliced

Pour cold Hawaiian punch into punch bowl. Add sherbet by scoopfuls; mix lightly. Float lemon and lime slices on top. May substitute raspberry sherbet for orange sherbet.

Yield: 30 servings.   **Prep Time:** 5 minutes.

PINK LASSIES

1 cup cranberry juice cocktail
¼ cup orange juice
1 cup vanilla ice cream

Process cranberry juice cocktail, orange juice and vanilla ice cream in blender until smooth and creamy. Pour into glasses.

Yield: 6 servings.   **Prep Time:** 5 minutes.

RED SATIN PUNCH

1 2-liter bottle of 7-Up
1 46-ounce can apple juice
1 32-ounce bottle of cranberry juice cocktail

Pour half the 7-Up into ice cube trays. Freeze until solid. Place 7-Up cubes in punch bowl. Pour remaining 7-Up, apple juice and cranberry juice cocktail over top, stirring to blend. Serve in punch cups.

Yield: 24 servings.   **Prep Time:** 5 minutes plus freezing.

SERENSIPITY

¾ cup sugar
1 cup half and half
Juice and grated rind of 1 lemon
1 1-liter bottle of 7-Up, chilled

Combine sugar, half and half, lemon juice and lemon rind in bowl; mix well. Spoon ¼ cup mixture into each glass. Fill with 7-Up; mix well. May substitute ginger ale for 7-Up.

Yield: 8 servings.   **Prep Time:** 5 minutes.

HEALTHY BANANA FRAPPÉ

1 cup orange juice
1 banana, sliced
2 ice cubes
½ cup low-fat vanilla yogurt

Combine orange juice, banana, ice cubes and yogurt in blender container. Process until smooth. May vary fruits, juices and amounts to suit personal preference.

Yield: 1 serving.   **Prep Time:** 5 minutes.

CHOCOBERRY YOGURT REFRESHER

1 cup strawberry yogurt   1 cup cold milk
1/2 cup sliced, fresh strawberries
3 tablespoons HERSHEY'S Chocolate Syrup
2 tablespoons light corn syrup   Crushed ice (optional)

Combine yogurt, milk, strawberries, chocolate syrup and corn syrup in blender container. Process until smooth. Serve over crushed ice if desired.

Yield: 3 servings.   **Prep Time:** 5 minutes.

Photograph for this recipe is on the cover.

CHOCOLATE CITRUS FLOAT

1 1/2 cups cold milk
1/4 cup frozen orange juice concentrate
3 tablespoons HERSHEY'S Chocolate Syrup
1 scoop vanilla ice cream
Crushed ice or additional ice cream (optional)

Combine milk, orange juice concentrate, chocolate syrup and ice cream in blender container. Process until smooth. Pour over crushed ice in glasses.

Yield: 3 servings.   **Prep Time:** 5 minutes.

Photograph for this recipe is on the cover.

LOW-CALORIE RASPBERRY MILK SHAKE

1/2 cup skim milk   1/2 cup plain low-fat yogurt
1 tablespoon sugar   1 teaspoon vanilla extract
1 cup frozen raspberries   Crushed ice

Combine skim milk, yogurt, sugar and vanilla in blender container. Process until smooth. Add frozen raspberries and crushed ice gradually, processing until slushy.

Yield: 2 servings.   **Prep Time:** 5 minutes.

STRAWBERRY YOGURT SHAKE

½ cup pineapple juice
1½ cups frozen unsweetened strawberries, thawed
¾ cup plain low-fat yogurt
1 teaspoon sugar

Combine pineapple juice, strawberries, yogurt and sugar in blender container. Process until smooth. Pour into glasses.

Yield: 2 servings.　　　　　　**Prep Time:** 5 minutes.

LUSCIOUS SLUSH

1 20-ounce can juice-pack crushed pineapple
1 6-ounce can frozen orange juice concentrate
1 banana, mashed
1 cup sugar-free ginger ale

Combine undrained pineapple and orange juice concentrate in blender container. Process until smooth. Add banana; mix well. Stir in ginger ale. Pour into 9x13-inch pan. Freeze for 30 minutes or until slushy. Spoon into glasses.

Yield: 4 servings.　　　**Prep Time:** 5 minutes plus freezing.

PEACH SLUSH

1 16-ounce package frozen peaches, slightly thawed
1 6-ounce can frozen orange juice concentrate
1 12-ounce can peach nectar
5 12-ounce cans lemon-lime soda, chilled

Combine peaches, orange juice concentrate and peach nectar in blender container. Process until smooth. Pour into ice cube trays. Freeze, covered, until firm. Let stand at room temperature for 20 minutes or until slightly thawed. Place 2 to 3 cubes and ½ can soda in each serving glass; stir gently until slushy.

Yield: 10 servings.　　　**Prep Time:** 5 minutes plus freezing.

FRUIT AND TEA PUNCH

3 cups sugar
Juice of 10 lemons   Juice of 2 oranges
1½ cups pineapple juice
4 quarts strong tea

Combine sugar, lemon juice and orange juice in punch bowl; mix until sugar is dissolved. Stir in pineapple juice and tea. Serve over crushed ice in glasses.

Yield: 20 servings.   **Prep Time:** 5 minutes.

FRUITED TEA

6 tea bags   2 quarts boiling water
¾ cup white grape juice
1 cup lemon juice   1½ cups sugar

Steep tea bags in water in large pitcher for 5 minutes. Remove tea bags. Add grape juice, lemon juice and sugar; mix until sugar is dissolved. Cool. Chill until serving time.

Yield: 12 servings.   **Prep Time:** 10 minutes plus chilling.

RASPBERRY TEA

1 large family-size tea bag
½ gallon boiling water
½ to ¾ cup sugar   1 lemon, sliced
1   64-ounce jar cran-raspberry juice

Combine tea bag and boiling water in pitcher. Steep until tea is strong. Remove tea bag. Add enough sugar to make sweeter than usual tea; stir until dissolved. Add lemon slices and cran-raspberry juice; mix well. Pour over ice ring in punch bowl. Ladle into glasses filled with ice. May microwave for 30 to 60 seconds and serve hot; do not boil.

Yield: 12 servings.   **Prep Time:** 10 minutes.

Hot Cranberry Cider

6 cups apple cider   4 cups cranberry juice cocktail
1/3 cup packed light brown sugar
Peel of 1/2 lemon   3 cinnamon sticks
1/4 teaspoon cloves

Mix apple cider, cranberry juice cocktail, brown sugar, lemon peel, cinnamon sticks and cloves in saucepan. Simmer for 30 minutes. Remove cinnamon sticks. Pour into cups.

Yield: 10 servings.   Prep Time: 5 minutes plus simmering.

Percolator Punch

1/2 cup packed brown sugar   4 cinnamon sticks
1 tablespoon whole cloves   1 tablespoon whole allspice
3 cups pineapple juice
2 cups cranberry juice cocktail   1 3/4 cups water

Combine brown sugar, cinnamon, cloves and allspice in percolator basket. Place pineapple juice, cranberry juice cocktail and water in percolator. Perk using manufacturer's instructions.

Yield: 8 servings.   Prep Time: 5 minutes plus perking.

Spiced Hot Tea

1 cinnamon stick   3 whole cloves
Nutmeg to taste
2 thin strips lemon peel
2 thin strips orange peel
4 cups water   3 or 4 tea bags

Combine cinnamon, cloves, nutmeg, lemon peel, orange peel and water in saucepan; mix well. Simmer for 10 minutes. Add tea bags. Steep until of desired strength; remove tea bags, fruit peels and whole spices. Serve hot.

Yield: 4 servings.   Prep Time: 15 minutes.

Cappucino Mix

1 8-quart package nonfat dry milk
1 16-ounce jar powdered coffee creamer
1 1-pound package instant cocoa mix
1 8-ounce jar instant coffee
1 1-pound package confectioners' sugar

Combine dry milk powder, coffee creamer, cocoa mix, instant coffee powder and confectioners' sugar in large container; mix well. Spoon 1/4 cup mixture into each mug. Add 1 cup boiling water, stirring until dissolved. Store mix in tightly covered container.

Yield: 32 servings.   **Prep Time:** 5 minutes.

Hot Cocoa Mix

2 cups powdered coffee creamer
2 cups sugar
3/4 cup instant cocoa mix
1 cup nonfat dry milk
1/4 teaspoon salt

Combine coffee creamer, sugar, cocoa mix, milk powder and salt in container; mix well. Spoon 2 to 3 heaping tablespoons mixture into each serving cup. Add 1 cup boiling water, stirring until dissolved.

Yield: 32 servings.   **Prep Time:** 5 minutes.

*Powdered coffee creamers and instant cocoa mix come
in low-fat but delicious versions.*

NUTRITIONAL INFORMATION

The editors have attempted to present these family recipes in a form that allows approximate nutritional values to be computed. Persons with dietary or health problems or whose diets require close monitoring should not rely solely on the nutritional information provided. They should consult their physicians or a registered dietitian for specific information.

Abbreviations for Nutritional Analysis

Cal — Calories	Dietary Fiber — Fiber	Sod — Sodium
Prot — Protein	T Fat — Total Fat	gr — gram
Carbo — Carbohydrates	Chol — Cholesterol	mg — milligrams

Nutritional information for these recipes is computed from information derived from many sources, including materials supplied by the United States Department of Agriculture, computer databanks and journals in which the information is assumed to be in the public domain. However, many specialty items, new products and processed foods may not be available from these sources or may vary from the average values used in these analyses. More information on new and/or specific products may be obtained by reading the nutrient labels. Unless otherwise specified, the nutritional analysis of these recipes is based on all measurements being level.

- **Buttermilk, sour cream** and **yogurt** are types available commercially.
- **Cake mixes** which are prepared using package directions include 3 eggs and 1/2 cup oil.
- **Chicken**, cooked for boning and chopping, has been roasted; this method yields the lowest caloric values.
- **Cottage cheese** is cream-style with 4.2% creaming mixture. Dry-curd cottage cheese has no creaming mixture.
- **Eggs** are all large.*
- **Flour** is unsifted all-purpose flour.
- **Garnishes**, serving suggestions and other optional additions and variations are not included in the analysis.
- **Margarine** and **butter** are regular, not whipped or presoftened.
- **Milk** is whole milk, 3.5% butterfat. Lowfat milk is 1% butterfat. Evaporated milk is whole milk with 60% of the water removed.
- **Oil** is any type of vegetable cooking oil. Shortening is hydrogenated vegetable shortening.
- **Salt** and other ingredients to taste as noted in the ingredients have not been included in the nutritional analysis.
- If a choice of ingredients has been given, the nutritional analysis information reflects the first option.

*To avoid raw eggs that may carry salmonella as in eggnog or 6-week muffin batter, use an equivalent amount of commercial egg substitute.

Pg #	Recipe Title (Approx Per Serving)	Cal	T Fat (g)	% Cal from Fat	Carbo (g)	Chol (mg)	Sod (mg)
14	Brownie Baked Alaska	424	18	36	63	39	169
14	Frozen Banana Split	653	39	52	70	70	236
15	Banana-Ice Cream Pie	357	16	39	51	22	357
15	Bubble Crown	231	14	55	22	98	124
16	Butter Brickle Dessert	379	17	40	54	10	182
16	Cherry Delight	454	27	51	53	32	268
17	Chocolate Ice Crispy Pie	341	15	38	50	44	218
17	Chocolate Malt Ice Cream Torte	360	17	42	47	41	233
18	Cranberry Ice Cream Pie	412	17	36	63	30	171
18	Easy Ice Cream Dessert	487	29	52	53	32	234
19	Crispy Ice Cream Roll	413	10	23	59	24	371
19	Mincemeat and Vanilla Ice Cream Torte	327	17	45	42	42	167
20	Mocha Parfait Pie	524	40	67	40	64	210
20	Orange Torte	555	23	35	88	51	159
21	Orange Sherbet Dessert	115	2	12	24	4	65
21	Peanut-Ice Cream Dessert	429	25	51	48	29	263
22	Peanut Buster Parfait	669	38	50	75	72	330
22	Frozen Piña Colada Ice Cream Dessert	207	15	61	18	20	62
23	Pineapple-Orange Parfaits	175	7	36	26	30	59
23	Pumpkin Ice Cream Pie	381	22	50	45	61	278
24	Rainbow Ice Cream Cake	320	7	20	60	30	314
24	Strawberries Romanoff	288	20	60	26	74	56
25	Giant Ice Cream Sundae	550	32	51	61	35	359
25	Oreo Sundae Dessert	552	33	54	57	36	357
26	Terrific Ice Cream Dessert	594	39	51	68	63	387
26	Thanksgiving Dessert	268	14	46	34	20	222
27	Frozen Christmas Bombe	418	22	45	55	68	80
27	Watermelon Bombe	229	5	18	47	11	67
28	Ice Cream Sandwich Dessert	230	12	45	30	0	29
28	Broiled Peaches Flambé	251	11	38	37	30	110
28	Vanilla Orange Delight	476	25	46	60	44	205
29	Cherry-Chocolate Chip Ice Cream	378	17	39	53	120	158
29	Cherry Mash Ice Cream	392	20	46	46	94	155
30	Strawberry Ice Cream	335	9	24	56	99	118
30	Oreo Ice Cream	462	31	60	39	178	153
30	Elegant Peachy Berry Sauce	90	<1	1	23	0	4
31	Exquisite Chocolate Sauce	159	8	40	25	18	35
31	Honey-Orange Cranberry Sauce	78	<1	2	21	0	1
32	Mexican Chocolate Sauce	223	12	45	30	43	57
32	Rich Caramel Sauce	221	13	54	25	33	69
34	Apricot Angel Cake	344	10	24	64	0	226
34	Apple Downside-Up Cake	234	8	31	37	27	443

Pg #	Recipe Title (Approx Per Serving)	Cal	T Fat (g)	% Cal from Fat	Carbo (g)	Chol (mg)	Sod (mg)
35	Granny's Applesauce Cake	318	11	29	56	28	418
35	Easy Banana Cake	214	2	10	46	0	319
36	Blueberry Tea Cake	572	25	39	81	100	389
36	Brown Sugar Cake	360	18	43	48	43	136
37	Microwave Carrot Cake	246	15	52	28	27	151
37	Chocolate Chip Cake	193	9	38	29	3	174
38	Chocolate Cheese Cupcakes	179	7	36	27	19	207
38	Mexican Chocolate Cake	443	19	38	68	1	284
39	Chocolate Cherry Cake	194	4	16	39	28	231
39	Chocolate Sundae Cake	446	18	35	70	0	236
40	Wacky Chocolate Cake	247	10	34	39	0	211
40	Coconut Cake	387	19	45	51	42	213
41	Cranberry Cupcakes	417	16	33	66	71	139
41	Fruitcake Cupcakes	173	7	33	29	4	31
42	No-Bake Fruitcake	311	12	33	51	13	201
42	Harvest Snack Cake	367	20	48	46	24	340
43	Hurry-Up Cakes	237	10	38	34	38	74
43	Ice Cream Cone Cupcakes	132	1	10	28	0	136
44	Lemon Angel Roll	400	11	24	73	16	218
44	Lemon Chiffon Cake	152	7	40	21	0	91
45	Mocha Pound Cake	421	30	62	37	96	237
45	Orange Cake	438	20	41	61	71	446
46	Old-Fashioned Cupcakes	153	5	30	24	30	104
46	Peanut Butter Cupcakes	150	5	28	25	13	124
47	Peach Preserve Cake	441	19	39	63	57	236
47	Sour Cream Peach Cake	158	4	22	29	24	176
48	Pear Cake	488	24	43	65	54	355
48	Microwave Pistachio Cake	335	16	41	46	60	269
49	Praline Cake	490	25	45	64	69	304
49	Pumpkin Cake Roll	315	17	47	38	79	226
50	Raspberry Jelly Roll	226	2	7	51	54	72
50	Sponge Cake	249	8	30	40	76	264
51	Strawberry Cake	409	25	53	44	57	252
51	Sunset Cake	398	23	52	45	53	342
52	Walnut Mocha Cake	340	24	61	30	90	76
52	White Grape Juice Cake	309	14	41	43	53	262
54	Almond Clusters	161	8	47	19	<1	114
54	Sweet and Spicy Almonds	156	12	66	10	0	202
55	Baby Ruth Candy	105	7	53	11	0	36
55	Bavarian Mints	129	8	50	16	6	22
56	Butterscotch Confetti	36	2	53	4	0	16
56	Caramel Fondue	109	5	42	15	11	71

Pg #	Recipe Title (Approx Per Serving)	Cal	T Fat (g)	% Cal from Fat	Carbo (g)	Chol (mg)	Sod (mg)
57	Microwave Caramels	60	3	40	9	1	25
57	Chocolate Chip Bonbons	111	6	49	14	5	15
58	Chocolate and Peanut Drops	97	7	64	6	0	11
58	Cherry Bings	87	6	54	9	1	37
59	Cherry Candy	228	10	37	34	2	103
59	Coconut Lemon Clusters	71	2	24	14	2	36
60	Coffee Creams	38	2	37	6	<1	19
60	Easy Peanut Butter Fudge	156	10	54	16	0	100
61	Haystacks	101	7	59	8	2	68
61	Kiss Candies	134	7	43	18	0	8
62	Chocolate-Covered Orange Slices	115	3	25	22	<1	16
62	Orange and Chocolate Truffles	101	7	57	11	6	44
63	Chocolate Peanut Clusters	115	8	56	10	3	51
63	Pecan Temptations	202	12	51	24	6	31
64	Pronto Pralines	150	7	41	22	2	43
64	Rocky Road Clusters	127	8	53	15	3	17
65	Tiger Butter	96	7	61	7	2	35
65	Microwave Toffee	190	10	44	28	0	49
66	Triple-Decker Fudge	72	4	43	10	4	16
66	Spiced Walnut Brittle	156	7	39	24	0	50
67	Chocolate-Covered Apples	294	16	45	42	3	15
67	Candy Hash	327	22	57	29	5	191
68	Caramel Crackers	333	14	37	47	0	595
68	Christmas Crunch	292	14	41	38	0	164
69	Quick Granola	364	14	32	58	<1	29
69	Easy Popcorn Balls	182	5	23	35	0	80
70	Popcorn Fantasy	150	8	48	19	0	81
70	Praline Nibbles	199	12	51	24	0	182
71	Light Iced Pretzels	33	<1	5	7	0	94
71	Sugar and Spice Snack	187	10	48	22	0	95
72	Sweet Crispmix	257	11	39	37	0	193
72	White Chocolate Crunch	147	8	45	19	3	144
74	Applesauce Raisin Cookies	133	6	37	20	10	128
74	Apricot Oatmeal Squares	183	8	39	26	9	116
75	Brownies	143	10	58	14	18	42
75	Black Forest Brownies	289	15	44	38	19	241
76	Caramel Squares	152	8	44	21	1	51
76	Cheesecake Squares	81	6	68	6	13	64
77	Cherry Winks	81	4	42	11	13	62
77	Chocolate Chip Cookies	158	9	48	20	12	132
78	Cranberry Tassies	127	8	55	13	14	77
78	Christmas Dollies	204	11	47	25	6	117

Pg #	Recipe Title (Approx Per Serving)	Cal	T Fat (g)	% Cal from Fat	Carbo (g)	Chol (mg)	Sod (mg)
79	Fruitcake Balls	113	6	43	16	2	8
79	Gingersnaps	51	2	39	7	3	24
80	Ice Cream Cookies	101	6	48	12	2	63
80	Lace Cookies	27	2	68	2	4	13
81	Ladyfingers	78	6	63	7	0	45
81	Lemon Bars	170	6	33	27	25	142
82	Mincemeat Squares	140	9	55	15	14	94
82	Molasses Drop Cookies	75	3	32	12	5	51
83	Grandma's Oatmeal Cookies	99	5	42	13	9	43
83	One-Cup Cookies	140	8	51	16	11	101
84	Magic Cookies	62	3	49	6	4	26
84	Peanut Butter Cookies	43	2	47	5	3	45
85	Pecan Dreams	155	7	37	24	0	14
85	Pineapple Hawaiian Kisses	72	6	67	5	0	55
86	Pistachio Icebox Cookies	37	2	42	5	3	18
86	Potato Chip Shortbread Cookies	92	6	56	10	0	58
87	Pumpkin Bars	344	17	44	46	56	121
87	Raspberry Thumbprints	130	8	51	15	26	5
88	Scottish Shortbread	321	19	52	36	25	193
88	Sesame Cookies	162	12	62	14	0	101
89	Snickerdoodles	46	2	40	6	10	37
89	Snickers Cookies	177	8	41	23	8	125
90	Sour Cream Cookies	52	2	39	7	5	30
90	Sugar Cookies	141	9	55	15	19	53
91	Old-Fashioned Tea Cakes	127	4	30	20	24	55
91	Toffee Bars	95	6	54	10	4	41
92	White Chocolate Chunk Cookies	91	5	46	11	5	46
92	Yum-Yum Bars	287	16	48	36	3	315
94	Almost Guilt-Free Dessert	174	5	22	33	2	33
94	Ambrosia Gratin	241	2	6	60	0	13
95	Apple Crisp	360	11	27	64	0	286
95	Creamy Coconut-Apple Crunch	268	12	39	39	19	280
96	Apple Dumplings	440	23	46	59	0	486
96	Creamy Apple Squares	256	13	44	35	21	310
97	Banana Split Dessert	416	27	56	45	0	317
97	Blackberry Fluff	353	17	42	48	14	74
98	Blueberry-Grape Compote	116	1	4	29	0	6
98	Midsummer Berries	372	22	53	42	53	255
99	Butterfinger Dessert	394	16	36	60	36	392
99	Lattice Cherry Cheesecake	514	28	15	350	103	380
100	Petite Cherry Cheesecakes	139	8	49	16	41	84
100	Chocolate Chip Cheesecake	420	29	59	36	94	297

Pg #	Recipe Title (Approx Per Serving)	Cal	T Fat (g)	% Cal from Fat	Carbo (g)	Chol (mg)	Sod (mg)
101	Mint Chocolate Chip Cheesecake	414	27	58	36	96	288
101	Chocolate Ribbon Cheesecake	390	30	66	27	46	285
102	Chocolate Turtle Cheesecake	438	28	57	42	73	267
102	Fudge Truffle Cheesecake	476	34	61	40	120	270
103	Pumpkin-Orange Cheesecake	463	31	59	39	109	376
103	Sour Cream Cheesecake	393	26	59	35	106	303
104	Cherries in the Snow	214	8	31	36	1	67
104	Cherry Dump Cake	360	16	38	54	0	367
105	Cherry Yum-Yum	379	19	43	52	19	332
105	Chocolate Dream Dessert	417	28	60	38	21	275
106	Chocolate Rice	178	<1	1	42	0	1
106	Blackberry Cobbler	256	3	12	53	0	205
107	Fruit Cobbler	291	13	39	42	27	233
107	Peach Cobbler	430	16	34	70	4	303
108	Sweet Potato Cobbler	476	21	39	72	0	312
108	Yummy Coconut Dessert	232	15	56	23	5	132
109	Cranberry Mousse	569	42	65	46	143	217
109	Date Nut Roll	239	6	22	45	1	201
110	Éclair Dessert	448	16	31	74	9	415
110	Mandarin Orange Dessert	285	15	45	36	9	218
111	Holiday Crown Dessert	496	32	57	47	62	195
111	Lemon Dessert	340	19	48	41	11	172
112	Peach Crumble	425	17	34	69	0	106
112	Peach Meringue with Raspberries	105	<1	1	26	0	20
113	Caramel Pears	204	11	47	28	27	59
113	Pineapple Delight	483	29	52	52	48	168
114	Banana and Berry Brownie Pizza	400	20	43	53	50	171
114	American Fruit Pizza	314	20	59	30	44	244
115	Delicious Banana Pudding	398	13	27	69	28	231
115	Brownie Pudding	278	4	14	59	26	176
116	Cherry Rice Custard Pudding	194	4	19	34	88	74
116	Doughnut Hole Custard Pudding	161	7	40	19	119	185
117	Old-Fashioned Egg Custard	150	6	35	21	84	73
117	Eggnog Rice Pudding	213	10	40	27	75	70
118	Frosty Pudding Cones	206	5	22	36	11	102
118	Delicious Pumpkin Dessert	519	32	54	56	11	242
119	Pumpkin Pie Squares	411	17	36	61	55	558
119	Punch Bowl Cake	273	11	34	43	18	190
120	Raspberry Swirl	435	30	60	39	56	194
120	Ritz Cracker Dessert	367	26	59	36	55	141
121	Danish Applesauce Torte	115	7	55	10	43	14
121	Make-Ahead Mocha Cream Torte	372	20	48	46	55	255

Pg #	Recipe Title (Approx Per Serving)	Cal	T Fat (g)	% Cal from Fat	Carbo (g)	Chol (mg)	Sod (mg)
122	Fantastic Chocolate Trifle	493	36	62	44	56	230
122	Light Strawberry Trifle	289	1	4	61	2	404
124	Microwave Apple Pie	416	19	40	60	39	287
124	Avocado Pie	555	36	56	55	13	295
125	Banana Cream Pie	303	11	33	46	86	183
125	Black Russian Pie	301	18	52	34	51	147
126	Fresh Blueberry Pie	325	19	51	39	41	152
126	Butterscotch Pie	370	17	42	50	88	315
127	Caramel Pies	538	26	43	75	11	314
127	Cherry Cream Cheese Pie	537	26	41	74	48	408
128	Chess Tarts	248	10	36	38	30	176
128	Chocolate Chess Pie	348	22	56	36	53	289
129	Chocolate Raspberry Tarts	630	45	61	58	62	193
129	Chocolate Truffle Pie	433	31	62	37	114	138
130	Microwave Coconut Pie	544	32	53	58	115	345
130	Coconut Cream Pie	544	32	52	59	117	278
131	Coffee-Almond Pie	417	29	62	32	119	189
131	Cranberry Mince Pie	431	16	33	70	2	361
132	Eggnog Chiffon Pie	262	13	46	29	109	189
132	Grapefruit Pie	283	8	23	53	0	172
133	French Silk Pie	601	45	63	51	42	480
133	German Mint Pie	444	29	56	46	41	261
134	Grasshopper Pie	340	19	50	42	41	217
134	Microwave Honey-Lemon Pie	403	27	59	33	65	144
135	Kiwi-Lime Pies	401	25	54	43	147	322
135	Lemon Pie	433	17	35	63	97	324
136	Sour Cream Lemon Pie	479	33	62	42	138	381
136	Key Largo Lime Tart	392	25	55	40	160	294
137	Luau Pie	336	20	53	37	21	264
137	Maple Syrup Pie	350	17	44	47	0	298
138	Mincemeat Chiffon Pie	437	25	50	49	121	288
138	Nutty Buddy Pies	434	25	51	49	12	339
139	Orange-Lime Pies	241	10	38	33	106	234
139	Pineapple Pie	273	11	34	43	53	274
140	Microwave Peach-Raisin Pie	389	15	34	64	0	301
140	Peanut Butter Pie	510	34	58	47	24	376
141	Pecan Caramel Tart	680	52	66	53	24	242
141	Pumpkin Chiffon Pie	459	30	58	46	82	208
142	Marshmallow and Strawberry Pie	393	17	38	59	3	317
142	Zucchini Pie	308	14	41	41	63	223
144	Instant Boiled Custard	166	5	27	26	20	142
144	Sparkling Christmas Punch	92	<1	0	23	0	5

Pg #	Recipe Title (Approx Per Serving)	Cal	T Fat (g)	% Cal from Fat	Carbo (g)	Chol (mg)	Sod (mg)
144	Easter Punch	35	<1	3	9	<1	6
145	Fruit Punch	58	<1	2	14	0	3
145	Lemon-Grape Punch	115	<1	1	29	0	12
145	Grape Juice Fizz	114	<1	1	29	0	16
146	Merry Berry Punch	62	<1	3	15	0	3
146	Mexican Punch	142	<1	2	37	0	2
146	Mock Piña Colada Punch	101	5	45	13	8	21
147	Orange Breakfast Nog	124	<1	2	26	2	64
147	Party Punch	154	1	6	37	4	62
147	Pink Lassies	74	2	29	12	10	20
148	Red Satin Punch	79	<1	1	20	0	11
148	Serensipity	162	3	19	33	11	26
148	Healthy Banana Frappé	313	2	7	68	6	78
149	Chocoberry Yogurt Refresher	230	5	18	43	11	103
149	Chocolate Citrus Float	200	7	29	31	26	87
149	Low-Calorie Raspberry Milk Shake	209	1	5	46	5	73
150	Strawberry Yogurt Shake	136	1	9	27	5	63
150	Luscious Slush	179	<1	2	45	0	8
150	Peach Slush	157	<1	1	40	0	24
151	Fruit and Tea Punch	137	<1	1	36	0	7
151	Fruited Tea	112	<1	1	29	0	6
151	Raspberry Tea	150	<1	0	38	0	14
152	Hot Cranberry Cider	162	<1	1	41	0	10
152	Percolator Punch	153	<1	1	39	0	10
152	Spiced Hot Tea	2	<1	6	1	0	7
153	Cappucino Mix	340	8	19	59	7	300
153	Hot Cocoa Mix	93	3	24	18	<1	43

Lighten Up!

Ingredients	Cal	T Fat (g)	% Cal from Fat	Carbo (g)	Chol (mg)	Sod (mg)
Cream Cheese (1-ounce)	98	10	87	1	28	86
* Light Cream Cheese (1-ounce)	62	5	67	2	16	160
Eggs (1)	79	6	64	1	213	69
* Egg Substitute (¼ cup)	25	0	0	1	0	85
Milk (1 cup)	150	8	49	11	33	120
* Skim Milk (1 cup)	86	<1	4	12	4	126
Whipped Cream (2 tablespoons)	52	6	93	<1	21	6
* Whipped Topping (2 tablespoons)	18	1	40	2	2	6
Sour Cream (1 tablespoon)	26	3	89	1	5	6
* Low-fat Yogurt (1 tablespoon)	9	<1	20	1	1	10

* Compare these ingredients to lighten up your recipes.

INDEX

FOR AVAILABLE BOOKS WITH ORDERING INFORMATION
Write to:
Favorite Recipes® Press
P.O. Box 305142
Nashville, TN 37230
or
Call Toll-free:
1-800-251-1542